DON BRADMAN · RICKY PONTING · AL-
GILCHRIST · KEITH MILLER · SHANE WARNE
MATTHEW HAYDEN · ARTHUR MORRIS · DO
BORDER · STEVE WAUGH · ADAM GILCHRIST
LILLEE · GLENN McGRATH · MATTHE
MAN · RICKY PONTING · ALLAN BORDER
MILLER · SHANE WARNE · DENNIS LIL
ARTHUR MORRIS · DON BRADMAN
WAUGH · ADAM GILCHRIST · KEITH M
nn McGRATH · MATTHEW HAYDEN · A
ONTING · ALLAN BORDER · STEVE WAU
ne WARNE · DENNIS LILLEE · GLENN M
ORRIS · DON BRADMAN · RICKY PONTI
ilCHRIST · KEITH MILLER · SHANE WA
MATTHEW HAYDEN · ARTHUR MORRIS · D
DER · STEVE WAUGH · ADAM GILCHRIS
LILLEE · GLENN McGRATH · MATTHE
MAN · RICKY PONTING · ALLAN BORDER
MILLER · SHANE WARNE · DENNIS LIL
ARTHUR MORRIS · DON
WAUGH · ADAM GILCHRIS
nn McGRATH · MATTHEW HAYDEN

The

IMMORTALS

of Australian Cricket

Liam Hauser

ROCKPOOL
PUBLISHING

A Rockpool book
PO Box 252 Summer Hill, NSW 2130

www.rockpoolpublishing.com.au
www.facebook.com/rockpoolpublishing

First published in 2018
Copyright text © Liam Hauser, 2018

ISBN 978-1-925682-78-6

A catalogue record for this book is available from the
National Library of Australia.

Cover design by Jessica Le, Rockpool Publishing
Editing by Lisa Macken
Internal design by Jessica Le, Rockpool Publishing
Typesetting by Typeskill
Images supplied by Newspix
Frontispiece image by the State Library of NSW of the Bardsley-
Gregory cricket team, 1930s.

Printed and bound in China
10 9 8 7 6 5 4 3 2 1

CONTENTS

INTRODUCTION

This task was never going to be easy. I knew it would be difficult to provide sufficient justification for many readers. Personally, I prefer to avoid trying to rank supposedly 'all-time greats' in sports, mainly because players who played many years apart simply cannot be compared for a myriad of reasons. All sports, let alone cricket, have undergone so many changes over the years that it is impossible to equate the merits or achievements of one player with another when they played in different eras.

Cricketers' careers are often judged according to their statistics – perhaps more so than most other sports – and this is one decisive factor in my selections. But, in saying that, is it possible to equate a batsman who averaged 50 in the 1960s to a batsman who averaged 50 in the 2000s? Of course not. There is no measure, or combination of measures, to make one's selections to the satisfaction of everybody. Even if there was, there would still be no guarantees that there would be uniformity among many people in their selections. Indeed,

Cricketers' careers are often judged according to their statistics . . .

I found myself leaning one way and then another way with many of my selections.

Undoubtedly some people would come up with a vastly different list from mine; some readers will surely wonder how I could have picked a certain player ahead of a different player. That doesn't mean to say I haven't considered players who other people would select. In fact, I really don't know how many players could be considered 'automatic selections' in everyone's choices. I would think probably only one or two.

The advent of limited overs cricket, the increasing amount of cricket played and the expansion of the number of competing countries are just some of the massive changes since Test cricket began in 1877. Protective equipment for batsmen has also improved a lot over the years – especially with regard to helmets – while other changes have included fielding restrictions, how many bouncers a bowler can deliver each over, the increase in power with the willow bats and more athleticism from players since the game became 'professional'. The introduction of the 'third umpire' and the technology available to adjudicate on numerous decisions have also brought about major changes.

That brings me to another debatable aspect of cricket that has been immensely modified, and that concerns uncovered pitches. For a long time now, pitches have been covered when rain intervenes, although this wasn't the case for many decades beforehand. What difference does this make? Well, I don't think there is an answer. Frankly, I find it bewildering (in fact, downright foolish) just how easily a lot of people jump to the conclusion that uncovered pitches automatically meant life became so much harder for batsmen and more favourable for bowlers. For starters, how often did rain affect the playing conditions during the years when pitches were uncovered? Did batting collapses often occur on sticky wickets? Was it solely because of the conditions? Why would sticky wickets always favour bowlers, when they had the challenge of handling a greasy ball while their run-up could also be hindered? It is quite clear to me that both batsmen and bowlers had difficulties – possibly

of equal measure – in the era of uncovered pitches.

There was a Test in 1935 in the Caribbean when treacherous conditions very much favoured bowlers. The West Indians were all out for 102 before England declared at 7-81, and then the hosts declared at 6-51. Set a target of 73, the tourists wobbled at 6-48 before winning by four wickets. Conversely, in the Ashes Test at Old Trafford in Manchester in 1902, Victor Trumper scored a century before lunch on the opening day, while England's strike bowler Bill Lockwood could not bowl for a while due to slippery footholds. As the thrilling Test – which Australia ultimately won by three runs – unfolded, there were batting collapses and recoveries as the weather fluctuated.

Put simply, I think uncovered pitches produced a lot of variables for batsmen and bowlers, while the same could be said about cricket when pitches were covered. It must also be said that the state of many pitches in various countries, regardless of the year and whether the pitch was covered or not, has often come in for criticism.

Back to my selection of the all-time greats. It must be made abundantly clear that there are no right or wrong choices, and that it is not necessarily possible to be fully comfortable with such a list. I will admit that, having started following cricket in 1990, I am naturally more inclined to favour – or at least have a greater understanding of the merits or otherwise of – players who have played since then. This is partly because some of them have set records, which admittedly has become somewhat easier to achieve than it was for players pre-1990 due to the vast increase in the amount of cricket being played. Rightly or wrongly, I sense that producing fine figures over an extended period of time against a broad range of opponents and in a broad range of countries tends to hold a player in higher stead than someone who played against notably fewer opponents and in a limited number of countries.

As I said earlier, statistics do not deserve to be the sole criteria for selection, but by the same token they can sway someone to lean one way or the other. Roland Perry's book *Bradman's Best Ashes Teams* – published in 2002, after Bradman's death the previous year – showed Bradman's tendency to favour players from his era. Would Bradman's selections be much different if he were still alive and made his selections when I put this book together? Who knows?

As for my selections, Bradman was an automatic choice – as I believe he would be for everyone. Widely regarded as the greatest batsman of all time, his average of 99.94 is a figure that will probably remain a standout forever. Yet there is no way of knowing what his record would have been had he played in another era. While a lot has been said about the infamous Bodyline Ashes series of 1932-33, I am not convinced that England's bowling attack was anywhere near as lethal or hostile as, say, a West Indian four-pronged pace attack in the 1980s. But therein lies the fact that it is simply not possible to compare players who played so many years apart.

Shane Warne and Adam Gilchrist were also automatic selections from my point of view and, I will admit, I followed their careers from start to end. I chose one specialist spinner in this list of players, and simply could not go past one of only two bowlers in Test cricket history who has topped 700 wickets. This meant there was simply no room for the likes of Bill O'Reilly, Arthur Mailey and Clarrie Grimmett. Gilchrist meanwhile broke wicketkeeping records, yet it is chiefly his batting that makes me select him. He became a much more prolific batsman than any of his predecessors, whether Australian or non-Australian, and his influence was immaculate as he effectively became the measuring stick for the role of a wicketkeeper-batsman. I acknowledge the fine glovework of other Australian wicketkeepers such as John 'Jack' Blackham, Don Tallon, Wally Grout, Rod Marsh and Ian Healy, but Gilchrist exceeded them considerably in the batting department while not necessarily paling much (if at all) in terms of wicketkeeping skills.

That leaves me trying to justify my selections of opening batsmen, the rest of the middle order and the fast bowlers. With opening batsmen, you could come up with a range of combinations as there are many candidates. I first chose Matthew Hayden because he averaged around 50, and changed the role of an opening batsman in terms of dominating rather than merely building a platform. Bill Lawry averaged in the high 40s but was overlooked partly because he hasn't often been referred to as a 'great' player, so to speak, and also because he lacked initiative. His very slow scoring made it hard for me to rank him highly enough. Bill Ponsford had a fine record but he played fewer than 30 Tests, and therefore had fewer opportunities than other candidates.

The player I chose was Arthur Morris who, admittedly, didn't have a career as long as he might have done due to World War II and for personal reasons. But he was a reliable batsman despite some lean trots (which even the great players have), and I found it notable that Bradman selected Morris in his best Australian Ashes team. Bob Simpson was another strong contender, while some would argue that Victor Trumper deserved a place. For all that has been said about Trumper, I couldn't rate him that high. His average of a shade under 40 makes good reading for someone who played very early in the 20th century, but I fail to see why he deserves to be ranked higher than other candidates.

The middle order has so many contenders, and it wasn't easy to omit the likes of Greg Chappell, Neil Harvey, Norman O'Neill, Stan McCabe and Charlie Macartney. I could not overlook Ricky Ponting after he finished his career as the second-highest run scorer in Test history, and repeatedly topped 1,000 runs in a calendar year. I also found it hard to overlook Allan Border, who played a huge role in reviving Australian cricket in the 1980s and starred when the rest of the team struggled on numerous occasions. Having played in an era that featured some ferocious West

Indian pace attacks, Border did brilliantly to average around 50, not to mention becoming Test cricket's highest run scorer at one point. His fielding and occasional left-arm spin bowling were also worthy assets.

Steve Waugh made the final cut after he also played a hugely influential role in Australian cricket, mainly after Border retired. As captain his record was excellent, while he was a very gutsy player who also averaged around 50 with the bat. His bowling became less frequent as his career progressed, but his fielding remained creditable and his batting was very consistent over a long period of time.

Keith Miller was a logical choice as an all-rounder as he had a fine record with bat and ball, thus pushing his claims above other contenders such as Warwick Armstrong, Richie Benaud, Ray Lindwall and Alan Davidson. This left room for two fast bowlers. Glenn McGrath was a relatively straightforward selection after notching more than 500 Test wickets and being a consistently big wicket-taker for well over a decade. Dennis Lillee was also a relatively straightforward selection, having spearheaded Australia's attack for many years and regularly being a prolific wicket-taker and inspiring a lot of youngsters with his aggressive

My team list could easily create many lively discussions . . .

style. Taking 355 wickets in 70 Tests makes outstanding reading, and Lillee would have had more than 400 wickets had he not played World Series Cricket in the late 1970s. Lillee has remained third on the list of Australian Test wicket-takers despite less Test cricket being played in his era compared with following eras. I could find no room for Fred 'The Demon' Spofforth, who also had outstanding figures yet played only 18 Tests, all of which were against England. It would have been interesting to see what he would have achieved if he had the chance to play more Test cricket, particularly against countries other than England.

I am open to hearing opinions from people as to why they would agree or disagree with my selections, as my list is not gospel or definitive. My team list could easily create many lively discussions, and it must be remembered that it is perfectly acceptable to agree to disagree.

Whether you agree with my all-time great Australian Test XI or not, I do hope you enjoy reading about some of the finest players in the history of cricket.

Matthew Hayden plays a cover drive during his century on day one of the Boxing Day Test against India in season 2007-08.

1

MATTHEW HAYDEN

Birth date	29 October 1971
Place of birth	Kingaroy, Queensland
Nickname/s	Haydos, Unit, Jurassic
Playing role	Left-handed opening batsman

An obscure yet highly commendable aspect of Matthew Hayden's cricket career is the fact he scored a century on his grade debut, and subsequently did likewise in his first-class debut and in his first match for Australia.

Yet after he played just one Test, in which he twice failed, there were suggestions that his Test career was over. As one of Australia's leading batsmen in the 1980s and early 1990s, David Boon, remarked with regard to Hayden in his 1996 autobiography *Under the Southern Cross*: 'Quite possibly, he may never play for his country again.'

Hayden's doubters were left with egg on their face as he ended up playing in more than 100 Tests and having more Test runs at a higher average than did Boon. On the back cover of Hayden's autobiography *Standing My Ground*, Steve Waugh is quoted as saying: 'No one ever gave Haydos any free passes.

He got there the hard way. The biggest accolade you can give a player is that they changed the perception of how a role should be played. Matthew took opening to a new level with his aggressive, dominating style. As a captain the greatest joy you can have is seeing a player fulfil his potential, which Haydos certainly did.'

In the introduction to the same book, Hayden commented: 'There were times when I felt unsupported and unrated, others when I felt I had almost too much support for my own good. I had one captain who didn't want me in his team, and others who made me feel as if they couldn't do without me.'

Hayden dives to make his ground during the first Test of the 2002-03 Ashes. Hayden scored 197 and 103 in this Test at the Gabba.

Steve Waugh, who captained Australia in 40 of the 103 Tests in which Hayden played, had a big influence on Hayden, including when Hayden was out of the Australian team: 'The greatest praise I can give to Stephen is to acknowledge that, without him, I wouldn't have succeeded at Test level. It really is that simple,' Hayden wrote in the chapter 'Waugh Games'.

Raised on a peanut farm in Kingaroy, Hayden played a lot of cricket at home with older brother Gary. Their first cricket pitch was homemade: mown and rolled in the backyard. After Gary left for boarding school, his younger brother often spent hours hitting a cricket ball that was tied in a stocking and hung from a pepperina

tree. Matthew Hayden's early interest in cricket escalated when, at the age of just seven, he attended a coaching camp held by former Queensland batsman Sam Trimble. Hayden played first-grade cricket in Kingaroy aged 15, remarking in his autobiography that 'playing against the big boys drove my competitive instincts'. Hayden moved to Marist College Ashgrove in Year 11 and was left out of the First XI, but he subsequently played club cricket for Valleys and was included in a Queensland under-17 side. Hayden was knocked back from the Australian Cricket Academy in

Hayden was knocked back from the Australian Cricket Academy in 1991 ...

1991 when head coach Rod Marsh told him something along the lines of: 'We're really only after players who are going to play first-class cricket.' Hayden had phoned Marsh, whose first two words were 'Matthew who?' Hayden went on to score 151 for Queensland's Second XI against the Academy, before being chosen for the start of the Sheffield Shield season. He scored 149 and 5 against South Australia in his first-class debut, shortly after his 20th birthday. A great career was in the making, but it took years for Hayden to prove that he could make the step up from domestic to international ranks.

Hayden (left) with team-mate Justin Langer (right) and then prime minister Paul Keating (centre), after Hayden and Langer opened the batting in a win for the Prime Minister's XI in a one-day match against a South African XI at Canberra's Manuka Oval in December 1993. Several years later, Hayden and Langer would establish a formidable opening pair for Australia in Test cricket.

The left-handed opener became the first player to notch 1,000 runs in his maiden first-class season, and the following season he also topped 1,000 first-class runs. Hayden consequently earned a place on the 1993 Ashes tour, where a spot was available to open the batting with the left-handed Mark Taylor, only for the right-handed Michael Slater to be picked ahead of Hayden. The Queenslander began the tour with 151 in a limited overs match against an England Amateur XI, and backed it up three days later with 122 against Middlesex in another 55 overs per side match. Hayden's maiden first-class match in England yielded scores of 3 and 96 against Worcestershire, but he struggled in his first three limited overs internationals as he tallied just 47 runs. Worse for Hayden, he scored just 2 and 15 while Slater made 91 and 50 not out in the last first-class match before the Ashes began. This may have swayed the selectors to pick Slater instead of Hayden for the Ashes, and Slater secured a berth as he and Taylor averaged in the low 40s. Hayden had to be content with becoming the first Australian to score 1,000 runs on tour without playing a Test, a worthy if bittersweet achievement. Hayden had a remarkable 1993-94 season, compiling 1,136 runs at 126.22 in six Sheffield Shield matches, yet his only appearances for Australia were irregular ones in the limited overs arena, in which his results were modest.

In Australia's 1994 tour of South Africa, Hayden was unprepared to make his Test debut in the opening match of the three-Test series. Taylor was a late withdrawal due to a virus, leading to Hayden being paired with Slater. After South Africa was dismissed for a disappointing total, Allan Donald and Fanie de Villiers gave Hayden a torrid time. Hayden made just 15 and 5 as South Africa won convincingly, and the Test debutant sustained a broken thumb from the second ball he faced in Australia's second innings. Taylor returned for the following Test, with the Taylor-Slater pairing looking like it could be entrenched for several years to come.

Hayden was picked for the second-string team called Australia A, a concept worth trialling but proving to be ill-fated in the 1994-95 World Series limited overs tournament. Hayden had an inconsistent season, but as time

went on he continued to knock on the door for Australian selection as he churned out the runs at domestic level. Slater was somewhat surprisingly dropped from the Australian line-up in late 1996, but Hayden remained on the outer as fellow left-hander Matthew Elliott was preferred. Hayden had made 224 and Elliott 158 in a tour match against the West Indians, then Elliott was omitted after two Tests due to a leg injury he sustained in a mishap when running between the wickets.

Curtly Ambrose, who hadn't played in the tour match, proved too much for Hayden, who failed miserably with 5 and 0 in his second

Hayden in action against the West Indies during the fourth Test at the Adelaide Oval in 1996-97. The Queenslander scored his maiden Test century in Australia's innings win to secure the Frank Worrell Trophy.

Test appearance. Ambrose missed the next Test with injury, and Hayden was reprieved a few times as he made a breakthrough 125 in Australia's innings victory. This sealed back-to-back series wins in the Frank Worrell Trophy.

In the dead rubber Test, Ambrose again dismissed Hayden for a duck before the Queenslander scored a gutsy 47 on a difficult deck in Australia's second innings. Subsequent scores of 40, 0, 14, 10 and 0 in South Africa were not enough for Hayden to keep his place in the team. In the Tests against the West Indies and South Africa, he was once bowled without offering a shot before twice being lbw without playing a stroke. He was also run out on one occasion in South Africa.

After missing out on the Ashes tour, Hayden played for Hampshire in 1997, scoring just 6 and 2 when Hampshire hosted the Australians. After being caught off Queensland team-mate Michael Kasprowicz, Hayden was bowled by Jason Gillespie – when shouldering arms. As Steve Waugh reported with regard to Hayden in *Steve Waugh's Ashes Diary* for 1997: 'His problems in this area will be another test

With Australia touring India soon afterwards, Hayden's career took a decisive turn.

for him to overcome, and how he recovers will be a good indicator of his mental fibre. I'm confident Matt will be back to play a vital role for Australia in the future, as he has a hunger and desire that very few others possess.'

Hayden again knuckled down at domestic level, but it was easy to think his Test career would not exceed seven appearances. Taylor and Elliott became Australia's opening pair, then Slater was recalled after Elliott lost form. Taylor's retirement in early 1999 created a vacancy, with Elliott recalled and again losing his way. Greg Blewett was then picked as an opener, after previously being in and out of the team when batting from three to six. Blewett was unable to maintain his place, and Hayden was recalled during a tour of New Zealand in 2000.

The sweep shot reaped a lot of runs for Hayden at Test level, starting in India in 2001.

Hayden scored 2 and 37 in the final Test against the Kiwis, before averaging a disappointing 29.50 with two half-centuries against the West Indies in five Tests at home in 2000-01. In the final Test, he was again lbw when padding away a ball that he thought would miss the stumps. 'I'd made starts, blown them, had some bad luck, made mistakes and been run out twice, including a heartbreaker at the Gabba just when I was beginning to blossom,' he wrote in his autobiography. Hayden conceded that early in his Test career he 'had been intimidated by that tortured feeling of extreme anxiety' before he batted, and that suddenly he 'was welcoming those stresses on board'. Hayden 'not only ceased to dread those stomach-churning emotions', but accepted he needed them as well.

With Australia touring India soon afterwards, Hayden's career took a decisive turn. He spent countless hours practising the sweep shot on a purposely prepared dry Brisbane deck before the Australians headed to the subcontinent. In the first Test, Hayden, by his own admission, played the sweep shot so often that he might as well have been playing with a broom (*Standing My Ground*, p. 168). Hayden scored 119 and 28 not out as Australia won the first Test by 10 wickets, and then he made 97 and 67 in the second Test, which India remarkably won after following on. Hayden's scores of 203 and 35 in the third Test weren't enough to prevent the hosts from winning the series, but the Queenslander's figures of 549 runs at 109.80 were more than double the next best Australian batsman's aggregate and average.

Hayden averaged just 33.42 in Australia's 4-1 Ashes triumph in England in 2001, yet the final Test began a new phase in his career. After Slater was dropped – never to be recalled – Justin 'Alfie' Langer was recalled; he was chosen to open after he had also been in and out of the team over a lengthy period. Langer usually batted at number three, but upon being recalled he scored 102 in his new position before retiring hurt. Hayden made 68 – his best score of the series – and the partnership produced 158 runs. Ultimately, the two left-handers compiled 5,655 runs from 113 innings when opening together. They notched six double century stands and eight other century stands.

Hayden utilises the sweep shot against the Indians on Australian soil in 2007-08.

In *The Ashes: Match of My Life,* Langer commented: 'We complement each other as batsmen, and understand each other because our careers have followed such similar paths. Batting with him in each Test is like going to Disneyland, we are like two little kids having the time of our lives.' In *Standing My Ground,* Hayden wrote that from their very first partnership they just clicked. Hayden considered they were united in their passion by their work ethic, but 'diametrically opposed in other areas ... We were the original good cop, bad cop. He'd be as smiling and happy as I

. . . it was something else to see him occasionally walk down the wicket in Tests intent on slamming the ball into the crowd.

was cold ... Alfie's great strength was my soft spot ... If we'd been rock groups, I was Hunters and Collectors and he was Nudgers and Deflectors ... Alfie's greatest skill was using the pace of the ball. Mine was being up and at the ball'.

Hayden plays a sweep shot against India at the Sydney Cricket Ground in January 2008. He made 13 and 123 in the tumultuous Test, which was marred by umpiring mistakes and unsporting conduct.

In *At the Close of Play*, Ricky Ponting commented: 'When Haydos was firing, which was most of the time between 2001 and 2008, no opening bat hit more powerfully through the line, or more often took control of the game from the jump. I batted No. 3, straight after him, so I often saw first-hand the sort of devastating impact he had on opposition bowlers.'

While Hayden could play efficient strokes all around the wicket and was adept at playing on both the front and the back foot, it was something else to see him occasionally walk down the wicket in Tests intent on slamming the ball into the crowd. It was a sign of belligerence, to say the least. When well set, Hayden was not only hard to dismiss but was determined to show he was in charge. As well as being a prolific run scorer, Hayden also proved to be a fine fielder in the slips and gully region.

After the Kiwis invited Australia to bat first in the opening two Tests of the Trans-Tasman series Down Under in late 2001, Hayden and Langer put on a double century stand in the first innings each time (although Langer was lucky not to be adjudged lbw in the opening

Hayden goes on the attack during his record-breaking Test innings of 380 against Zimbabwe at Perth in October 2003.

over of the first Test). Hayden scored 136 on the opening day of the first Test, and finished the series with 297 runs at 59.40. As Australia subsequently hosted South Africa for three Tests before the Proteas hosted three Tests, Hayden struck a purple patch that should forever remain entrenched as one of the best patches of form by a Test batsman.

The Australians won the first five of those Tests and lost the last one. Hayden's scores were 31, 131, 138, 3 not out, 105 and 21 not out in Australia, followed by 122, 63, 96, 28 and 0 in South Africa. His 122 was part of a total of 7-652 declared as it was Allan Donald's last Test, with the South African paceman proving barely a shadow of his former self. Having fallen four runs shy of a century in Australia's second innings of the following Test, Hayden narrowly missed out on achieving a triple-figure score in five successive Tests.

Hayden relished playing an Ashes series on home soil for the first time in 2002-03. The first Test was on his home turf in Brisbane, where he made a memorable double of 197 and 103. He notched one more ton in the series. Like any

batsman, Hayden sometimes failed and sometimes made starts without converting them into big scores, but his tendency to score strongly on a regular basis enabled him to top 1,000 Test runs in each calendar year from 2001 to 2005.

Hayden scored two tons in his first Test series in the Caribbean – a four-match series in the first half of 2003 – before creating a world record in October 2003. Against Zimbabwe at Perth he scored 380, which bettered Brian Lara's 375 as the highest individual Test score; Lara regained the record with a score of 400 not out. Hayden's phenomenal innings contained 38 fours and 11 sixes, as he faced 438 balls in 622 minutes. In the following Test, Hayden notched an unbeaten 101 as Australia coasted to another easy win.

Hayden was second to Ponting in Australia's run making in the 2003-04 drawn series with India, before Australia hosted Sri Lanka for two Tests in the winter of 2004. Hayden achieved two centuries in a Test for the second and last time. Again he was in his home state, albeit this time in Cairns: his scores were 117 and 132.

Hayden's form tapered off during the latter part of 2004, and his troubles continued in the 2005 Ashes. He averaged just 22 in the first five Tests, having been repeatedly dismissed for scores between 26 and 36; reverse swing was troubling the Australians. A score of 138 in the final Test saved Hayden's place in the side, before he made a fine double of 111 and 77 in a Test against a World XI in Sydney. In a 3-0 whitewash of the West Indies on Australian turf, Hayden scored 37, 118, 110, 46, 47 and 87 not out, with tons in the first two Tests enabling him to achieve four centuries in as many Tests for the second time. Against South Africa he began with 0 and 20, before rattling off scores of 65, 137, 4 and 90 in a 2-0 series win.

In a subsequent 3-0 series win on South African soil, Hayden had an up-and-down time with scores of 94, 32, 0, 102, 3 and 0. In his final Ashes series, in 2006-07, Hayden must have felt frustrated as his first five scores were between 12 and 37, then he fell eight runs shy of a century in Australia's second innings at Perth. Hayden made 153 in an innings win in Melbourne, before scoring 33 and 23 not out in Sydney. In the final

But there was little doubt that as his form had lapsed the end was nigh.

Test he hit the winning runs to seal a 5-0 whitewash in the last Test for Shane Warne, Glenn McGrath and Hayden's great mate Langer, who was at the non-striker's end.

Hayden was unable to make a big score in three knocks against Sri Lanka in late 2007, then against India he made scores of 124, 47, 13, 123 and 103. Australia beat Sri Lanka 2-0 and then accounted for India 2-1, with an injured Hayden missing the third Test against India when the tourists had their sole victory of the series. Hayden's third ton of the series turned out to be his final Test century, and he finished with slightly more centuries than half-centuries: it should be noted that several of his half-centuries were scores in the 90s.

Hayden's career drew towards a close in season 2008-09, not long after he turned 37. He was a little unlucky on occasion when Australia toured India and hosted New Zealand and South Africa, having once been ruled caught-

and-bowled when the ball touched his pad only and run out a couple of times. But there was little doubt that as his form had lapsed the end was nigh. With several other high-profile Australian players having retired within the past two years, the Australians somewhat failed to maintain their high achievements. They lost 2-0 in India, where Hayden struggled at first – scoring two ducks and tallying just 42 runs in his first four digs, before making scores of 83, 16 not out, 16 and 77. In a 2-0 whitewash of the Kiwis, Hayden failed with 8, a first-ball duck and 24.

The only occasion Hayden was in a losing series on home soil was his farewell series, although it was not known until late in the series that Hayden would soon retire from first-class and international cricket. He scored 12, 4, 8 and 23 as the hosts tumbled to an insurmountable 2-0 deficit, before Australia at least won his final Test, in which he scored 31 and 39.

In limited overs internationals, Hayden averaged 26 in 13 matches across 1993 and 1994 before being on the outer for almost six years. His maiden one-day international century came during his excellent tour of India in 2001, nearly eight years after his international debut. Even during his sparkling vein of form in the Test arena in 2001-02, Hayden was yet to cement a place in the one-day line-up. When he finally nailed a permanent berth he formed a formidable partnership with another left-hander, Adam Gilchrist. The duo sought to flay the bowling from the outset. Hayden temporarily held the highest individual one-day score by an Australian, scoring 181 not out against New Zealand at Hamilton in early 2007. Hayden was also involved in Australia's 2003 and 2007 World Cup wins, and in the 2007 final against Sri Lanka he scored just 38 in a match-winning opening stand of 172 in just 22.5 overs.

A devoted Catholic, Hayden acknowledged a contradiction in the way he conducted himself in the cricketing arena. He crossed his chest each time he posted a Test century, yet was also chiefly involved in Australia's notorious sledging. In the introduction of his autobiography, Hayden remarked: 'Was I a hypocrite? Maybe. But I am what I am: a man of contradictions. There's the real me, and then there's the person many people think I am. I'm the kind of person who needs to be in control. Perhaps that's why I gravitated towards being an opening batsman. There's a degree of certainty that comes with the role.' Later, Hayden said he was 'often accused of being too arrogant', yet there was one occasion when Allan Border accused him of being too timid.

Away from cricket, Hayden was renowned for enjoying cooking, surfing and fishing as hobbies. He has had three cook books published.

Career statistics

	Tests	One-day internationals	First-class matches
Matches	103	161	295
Innings	184	155	515
Not outs	14	15	47
Runs scored	8,625	6,133	24,603
Batting average	50.74	43.81	52.57
100s / 50s	30 / 29	10 / 36	79 / 100
Top score	380	181*	380
Balls bowled	54	6	1,097
Runs	40	18	671
Wickets	-	-	17
Bowling average	-	-	39.47
5 wickets in an innings	-	-	-
10 wickets in a match	-	n/a	-
Best bowling	0 / 7	0 / 18	3 / 10
Catches	128	68	296

Hayden celebrates one of many milestones during his marathon 380 against Zimbabwe.

The pull shot was one of Arthur Morris'
specialties in his 46 Tests for Australia.

2

ARTHUR MORRIS

Birth date	19 January 1922 (died 22 August 2015)
Place of birth	Bondi, Sydney, New South Wales
Nickname/s	None
Playing role	Left-handed opening batsman

Were it not for the intervention of Bill O'Reilly, Australia's renowned leg-spinner who played Test cricket from 1932 to 1946, Arthur Morris could have had a very different career from what unfolded. What that might have entailed is anyone's guess.

Perhaps the highlight of Morris' career, and one of the chief reasons he earned selection in this list of Australian cricketing immortals, was leading the Test batting aggregates and averages in Australia's famous 'Invincibles' tour of England in 1948. Averaging in the mid to high 40s as an opening batsman in the 1940s and 1950s was a huge achievement, after World War II impeded his development as a cricketer and delayed his introduction to the Test arena. Additionally, Morris' career was cut short when his wife contracted terminal cancer.

Morris' career figures reveal that he scored as many centuries as half-centuries in Tests (12 of each), and an equal number of centuries and half-centuries in first-class cricket (46 of each). In first-class cricket for New South Wales, he scored 17 centuries and 17 half-centuries while averaging 63.84 from 50 appearances. A lesser-known fact was that Morris scored a century on debut in four countries: Australia, England, South Africa and the West Indies.

Morris played a range of sports, including cricket, rugby union and tennis, in his childhood and

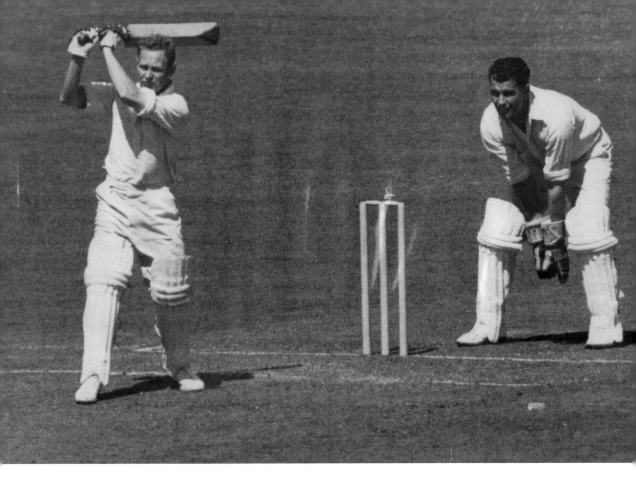

Morris drives confidently.

Perhaps the highlight of Morris' career . . . was leading the Test batting aggregates and averages in Australia's famous 'Invincibles' tour in 1948

teenage years. He lived in Bondi, then Dungog, then Newcastle and returned to Sydney in his childhood. In Sydney club cricket at under-16 level he captured 55 wickets at a staggering average of 5.24 in one season with his left-arm chinaman bowling, yet captain O'Reilly deemed that Morris' bowling would not enable him to go very far. Morris was promptly promoted to number six in the batting order, then he was promoted to opener after making a triple-figure score.

Aged 18, Morris was an instant success as a left-handed opening batsman in his first-class debut. Playing for New South Wales against Queensland, he gave an early chance in both innings, but nothing could detract from his scores of

148 and 111 as he became the first player to score two centuries on debut in first-class cricket. In the first innings, he added 261 runs with the right-handed Sid Barnes, who scored 133 at number three, and this duo would later open the batting in Tests. In the second innings, Morris and opening partner Morton Cohen put on an opening stand of 200. 'The cricket world sat up and took notice,' Roland Perry reported in *Bradman's Best Ashes Teams* with regard to Morris in his first-class debut. 'Such a display revealed several things. First, the cricketer most likely had the right mental strength for big cricket. Second, his powers of concentration were clearly exceptional. Even the great and most experienced among batsmen in history rarely came up twice with such force and determination in one match.'

Morris could well have made the Test team at the age of 18 or 19 had World War II not intervened. Morris enlisted in the Australian Imperial Forces, and was stationed in New Guinea as well as his home country. Morris played more rugby union than cricket during these years, before returning to first-class cricket

Morris could well have made the Test team at the age of 18 or 19 had World War II not intervened.

in 1946-47. Keith Miller tested Morris with a series of bouncers in one over during a Sheffield Shield match at the Sydney Cricket Ground, and Morris replied with a series of hook shots as 24 runs came off the over.

Morris was selected for that season's Ashes series Down Under, following a fine 115 for an Australian XI against the Marylebone Cricket Club. But Morris' first two Tests must have been immensely frustrating for him as he spent much of the time watching team-mates pile on the runs. Chosen to open with Barnes, Morris encountered a particular bowler who troubled him time and time again as his career unfolded. Morris scored just 2 when seam and swing bowler Alec Bedser had him caught in the slips from a ball that swung away from the left-hander.

Having won the toss and chosen to bat first in the Brisbane Test, Don Bradman went on to score 187 while Lindsay Hassett scored 128 in an Australian total of 645 before the hosts won by a staggering margin of an innings and 332 runs.

The second Test at Sydney had something of a similar theme, albeit after England batted first. Morris played a delivery from Bill Edrich on to the stumps after scoring 5, before Bradman and Barnes scored 234 each to set up another innings victory. Morris made a better start to the third Test at Melbourne, scoring 21 before Bedser had him lbw. The second innings proved a revelation as Morris compiled 155, having struck only eight fours in his 364-minute stay before Bedser bowled him. The Melbourne Test was drawn, as was the fourth Test at Adelaide, where Morris strengthened his credentials by scoring 122 and an unconquered 124 while England's Denis Compton made 147 and 103 not out.

Continuing a pattern, Bedser claimed Morris' wicket in the first innings at Adelaide before doing likewise in the fifth Test at Sydney. Morris made 57 in Australia's first innings and was run out in the second innings, with the hosts wrapping up a 3-0 series win with a five-wicket victory as the target was 214. Morris' series figures of 503 runs at 71.86 were second only to Bradman's 680 at 97.14.

Australia's next Test assignment was a five-match home series against India the following summer, with the hosts winning all bar the second Test as it was India's first series on Australian soil. Morris was bizarrely out hit wicket after scoring 47 in the first Test, which Australia won by an innings. Morris' best Test in the series was the third at Melbourne, where he made 45 and 100 not out, having batted at number five in the second innings after Ian Johnson and Bruce Dooland opened when the batting line-up was reshuffled. Morris finished third in the Australian aggregates, with 209 runs at 52.25. He was omitted from the final Test as his position in the 1948 England tour was secure, and his replacement Bill Brown was run out for 99 while Barnes was run out for 33. Australia topped 500 and won by an innings for the third time in the series.

The tour of the Invincibles was the first time Morris played Test

cricket overseas, and Bradman rated him so highly that Morris was chosen as an on-tour selector along with Hassett and Bradman himself. Morris' aggregate of 1922 first-class runs at 71.18 was second to Bradman's 2428 at 89.92. In the Test arena, Morris was the only player to record three centuries as he tallied 696 runs at 87; Bradman was Australia's next best, with 508 at 72.57. Morris made 138 against Worcestershire in his first match on tour but had an ordinary start to the Ashes series, being twice bowled in the first Test with Bedser the bowler on the latter occasion.

Morris made 105 and 62 in the second Test while opening partner Barnes made 0 and 141, and then Morris made his highest first-class score of 290 against Gloucestershire. Morris followed up with two 50s in the third Test.

The fourth Test at Headingley was memorable for Morris, as Australia achieved a target of 404 for the loss of just three wickets. England flopped for 496 after being 2-423, and then Australia was 1-13 as Morris was caught off Bedser for 6. In the run chase, Hassett's departure left the tourists 1-57 before Morris and Bradman set up

Morris (third from right) at a reunion of the 1948 Invincibles team.

the victory with a 299-run stand, with Morris scoring 182 and Bradman an undefeated 173.

In the fifth Test at the Oval, where Bradman bade farewell to Test cricket, Morris was unfortunate not to make a double century, being run out for 196. Remarkably, this innings has largely faded into obscurity due to Bradman's second-ball duck: Bradman needed just four runs in his final Test innings to finish with an average of 100. Morris was undoubtedly asked a number of times if he had witnessed Bradman's final Test innings, those asking the question obviously not being aware

that Morris had been at the non-striker's end and on his way to 196.

Indeed, it was one of two noteworthy instances when Morris was at the non-striker's end. The first instance was in the second Test against India in late 1947, when Vinoo Mankad ran out Bill Brown at the bowler's end before the bowler delivered the ball. Ironically, Mankad had warned Morris but not run him out for a similar transgression in the previous Test, before this mode of dismissal was named after the bowler who ran out Brown.

Following Bradman's retirement, Morris became vice-captain, while

Morris pulls the ball behind square during a Test against India in late 1947.

Morris (right) with Australian opening batsman Mark Taylor in the late 1980s.

Hassett was captain for Australia's 1949-50 tour of South Africa. After starting with a ton against Natal, Morris scored a duck in the first Test before a century in each of the last two Tests lifted his series figures to 422 runs at 52.75. Australia won the five-match series 4-0. As hosts, Australia won the 1950-51 Ashes 4-1, having lost the last Test. Morris was one of four Australians to score between 321 and 366 runs but he struggled for much of the time, with Bedser dismissing him five times. Morris' only notable innings was in the fourth Test at Adelaide, where he made his best Test score of 206 to set up a total of 371.

Morris' most disappointing Test series was at home against the West Indies in 1951-52, as he didn't even manage a half-century and averaged just 23.25 in the first four Tests before missing the fifth with injury.

Morris was one of four Australians to score between 321 and 366 runs but he struggled for much of the time . . .

He found spin rather than pace the most problematic, as Alf Valentine and Sonny Ramadhin dismissed him repeatedly. Australia won the series 4-1, with Morris leading the team in its six-wicket defeat at Adelaide as Hassett was sidelined.

Morris was also below his best as hosts Australia had to settle for a 2-all drawn series with South Africa in 1952-53, after Australia twice moved to a series lead. Morris was unable to convert starts into big scores, tallying 370 runs at 41.11, and in the final Test he was a run-out sacrifice for 99. The other batsman, fellow left-hander Neil Harvey, went on to score 205, but Australia lost by six wickets after having the upper hand at various stages. Morris meanwhile claimed his first Test wicket with his scarcely used bowling, bowling John Watkins during the drawn fourth Test.

Morris also made regular decent starts without turning any of them into a triple-figure score in the 1953 Ashes series, with England winning the urn for the first time since the infamous Bodyline series a little over 20 years earlier. Bedser dismissed him once in each of the five Tests, and Morris claimed his second and final Test wicket when he bowled Bedser in the third Test. Morris failed miserably with the bat, scoring 1 and 0.

The return series in Australia barely 18 months later started brilliantly for Morris. He made his first Test ton for nearly four years, compiling 153 at Brisbane and helping to set up an Australian victory by an innings and 154 runs. Morris suffered a battered and bruised body in the process as he often didn't use his bat to fend off bouncers – particularly from Frank Tyson, who took 1-160. Bedser, who took 1-131, was omitted for the remainder of the series, while Morris was appointed to lead Australia for the second and final time in Tests as Ian Johnson and Keith Miller missed the second Test at Sydney due to injury. Unfortunately for Morris,

> Morris suffered a battered and bruised body in the process as he often didn't use his bat to fend off bouncers . . .

he scored just 12 and 10, while his Test captaincy record yielded two losses from as many Tests.

Morris' team had a 74-run first innings lead, but lost by 38 runs when seeking 223 as Tyson completed a 10-wicket match haul. After missing the final Test, Morris' series figures of 223 runs at 31.86 were disappointing, although the only Australian to better him with the bat was Neil Harvey with 354 at 44.25, as England turned a 1-0 deficit into a 3-1 triumph.

Morris' final Test series was in the Caribbean in 1955, with the Australians winning 3-0 after Morris began the tour with a century against Jamaica. His Test scores were 65, 1, 111, 44 and 38 although he missed the fourth Test, and in his final Test he batted at first drop and scored 7. It was the third time in

Tests that he hadn't opened, having twice batted at number five.

Morris' last Test resembled his first two, with him spending a lot of time in the pavilion watching his team-mates set up a mammoth total; the Australians needed to bat only once. Five of Morris' team-mates scored tons in his farewell, with Harvey top scoring with 204 and Australia amassing 8-758 declared and winning by an innings and 82 runs despite two tons from West Indian Clyde Walcott.

Morris was only 33 when he played his final Test, giving up first-class cricket because his wife Valerie had breast cancer. She died at the age of 33 after just 18 months of marriage. Morris remarried in 1968.

Morris has earned plenty of compliments over the years, as much for his personal qualities as for his cricketing qualities. In a profile of Morris on *Cricinfo*, Gideon Haigh introduced with the words: 'The acme of elegance and the epitome of sportsmanship.' Also on *Cricinfo*, Neil Harvey said he learned a lot from Morris over the years: 'A better bloke you couldn't find,' Harvey said. In *The Illustrated Encyclopedia of World Cricket*, Peter Arnold wrote: 'Arthur Morris could be called

Morris pulls authoritatively during a contest in the 1950s.

'Perhaps Morris's most important sign of genius was his capacity to impose his will on a big or important occasion.'

"The Quiet Australian". A pleasant, modest, and kind man, he was liked wherever he went … In keeping with his manner, Morris was more of a gentle persuader of runs rather than an aggressive acquirer … A player of complete calm with a sound defence and neat style, he excelled in placing his strokes wide of fieldsmen, and often he would upset bowlers by walking down the pitch and putting them off their length.' Alan Davidson remarked on *Cricinfo*: 'You had to see the bloke and his artistry, his ability was phenomenal. It didn't matter if it was a fast bowler or a spin bowler. He'd go down the wicket to a spinner and pick them off. He was a magnificent back-foot player. His judgement of the length of a ball was incredible.'

In *Bradman's Best Ashes Teams*, Bradman summed up Morris thus:

'His most outstanding quality was plenty of time to play his shots. He could drive, glance, hook and cut. All were executed with the same facility. Arthur was a wonderful player to watch from the beginning of an innings. He often set the tone for a game. He wasn't always straight in defence. But this was merely a sign of genius. He rarely, if ever, got out from this. Arthur had an ideal temperament.' Perry went on to write in the same book: 'Perhaps Morris's most important sign of genius was his capacity to impose his will on a big or important occasion. This applied to scoring a century when first playing a foreign country and to performing at his best in a series-deciding Test. Bradman appreciated this quality immensely.'

Career statistics

	Tests	One-day internationals	First-class matches
Matches	46	-	162
Innings	79	-	250
Not outs	3	-	15
Runs scored	3,533	-	12,614
Batting average	46.49	-	53.68
100s / 50s	12 / 12	-	46 / 46
Top score	206	-	290
Balls bowled	111	-	718
Runs	50	-	592
Wickets	2	-	12
Bowling average	25	-	49.33
5 wickets in an innings	-	-	-
10 wickets in a match	-	-	-
Best bowling	1 / 5	-	3 / 36
Catches	15	-	73

Don Bradman shows his classical poise and style while playing a drive.

3

DON BRADMAN

Birth date	27 August 1908 (died 25 February 2001)
Place of birth	Cootamundra, New South Wales
Nickname/s	The Don
Playing role	Right-handed middle order batsman

There is little doubt many people consider it an indisputable fact that Don Bradman was far and away the greatest batsman in the history of cricket. Certainly from a statistical perspective Bradman's feats are not only unmatched but also unapproached, his Test batting average being a smidgen below 100.

It is somewhat ironic that he has been well remembered for scoring a duck in his final Test innings to leave him with an average of 99.94, yet in no way did it lessen his greatness.

Apart from raw statistics, perhaps the most staggering aspect of Bradman's career was that he barely went through a bad trot with the willow. At no stage could he have been considered out of form, and it became apparent that opponents could ill-afford to think he was due for a failure. Even though Bradman scored seven ducks in his 80 Test innings, he scored at least one century in each of the 11 Test series in which he played, scoring a ton 36.25 per cent of the time and a half-century 16.25 per cent of the time. He was not only capable of turning a 50 into a century, but also more than capable of going on to 150 and beyond.

Bradman's ability to regularly notch huge scores suggested he had amazing concentration as much as batting ability. As Peter Arnold reported in *The Illustrated Encyclopedia of World Cricket*: 'The physical attributes and the

A portrait of Bradman in 1929.

. . . Bradman scored his first ton in school cricket when he was 12 years old.

astonishing co-ordination that produced his peerless batting were supported by a temperament combining great application, an intense sense of purpose, and a streak of ruthlessness.'

Bradman scored two triple centuries at Test level, and on 10 other occasions he scored a double century. His lowest series average was 56.57 while his second-lowest was 66.86, figures that could only be considered modest by Bradman's standards when looking at his overall record. It remains a matter of conjecture as to how Bradman would have fared had he played in another era such as that involving professional cricket, including limited overs matches, and if he had played at Test venues other than in Australia and England. He can only be judged according to when and where he played. He certainly stood head and shoulders above everyone else when it came to batting feats and figures.

Well known for using a cricket stump to hit a golf ball against a water tank during his childhood, Bradman scored his first ton in school cricket when he was 12 years old. When filling in for the local Bowral team in late 1920, he made undefeated scores of 37 and 29 on debut. His father took him to the Sydney Cricket Ground that season to watch the fifth Ashes Test, which fuelled an ambition in the young Bradman to play at that venue in the future. Bradman worked for a real estate agent and, incredibly, gave up cricket for two years before resuming in 1925-26, attracting attention from the Sydney press for his big scoring in rural matches. He was invited to play for St George in Sydney, and immediately impressed with his first century on a turf wicket. For a little while, Bradman travelled the 130-odd kilometres from Bowral to Sydney each Saturday to play for St George.

Bradman in front of the grandstand that was named after him at the Adelaide Oval, in January 1990.

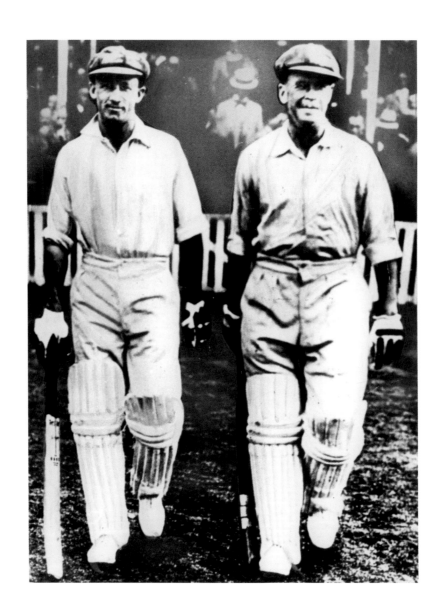

Bradman with Bill Ponsford in 1934.

Bradman made his first-class debut in December 1927. The 19-year-old was an instant success, scoring 118 and 33 for New South Wales against South Australia at Adelaide, batting first at seven and then at six. He was a little patchy in the next few games, and scored 0 and 13 at number eight against Queensland before scoring 134 not out against Victoria at Sydney. At the start of the following season Bradman made a huge impact against Queensland, scoring 131 in a total of 248 and then 133 not out as New South Wales won by six wickets when chasing a 399-run target.

Promptly catapulted into the Test team for the 1928-29 Ashes, Bradman made just 18 and 1 on debut at Brisbane. England won by 675 runs after the hosts crumbled for 122 and 66. Having batted at seven and six on debut, Bradman was dropped for the second Test but recalled for the third at Melbourne, where England won by three wickets to seal the series. Bradman secured his place in the Australian team with scores of 79 and 112 at number six in his second Test appearance. In his fourth Test, which was also at the Melbourne Cricket Ground, Bradman made 123 and 37 not out;

Australia won by five wickets to avoid a 5-0 whitewash. In the lead-up to his third Test, Bradman scored 340 not out against Victoria in a Shield match at Sydney.

Bradman made his highest first-class score the following season when he compiled 452 not out for New South Wales against Queensland at Sydney. Interestingly, he opened in the first innings and departed for 3 before batting at first drop in the second innings. Alec Hurwood, who had Bradman caught behind in the first innings and claimed 10 wickets in the match, reported years later that he 'bowled' Bradman for 80 in the second innings but that the bails were not dislodged. The fortunate Bradman subsequently reached 100 in 104 minutes, 200 in 185 minutes, 300 in 288 minutes and 400 in 377 minutes, then batted for a further 38 minutes before captain Alan Kippax declared the innings closed at 8-761. It was anyone's guess as to what Bradman would have scored had he batted until dismissal. The tiring Queenslanders were generous enough to chair him from the field, before collapsing to 84 all out as the hosts recorded a 685-run victory.

In Australia's subsequent tour of England for the 1930 Ashes –

Bradman signs a cricket bat during an interview with television reporter Ray Martin.

Bradman's second series in Test cricket – spectators were treated to what was surely the best exhibition of batting until that time. Bradman batted seven times in the five Tests and chalked up a staggering 974 runs at an average of 139.14. He batted at number four in the first innings of the first Test and then cemented his place in the number three slot, where he usually batted thereafter.

After scoring 8 and 131 in a 93-run loss at Trent Bridge, Bradman scored 254 and 1 in a seven-wicket triumph at Lord's. His peak was the third Test at Headingley, where he made his highest Test score of 334. He amazingly scored 105 in the first session, 115 in the second session and then progressed to 309 at stumps. The Headingley Test was drawn, as was the fourth at Old Trafford, where Bradman made 14. The tourists won the deciding Test at the Oval, following 232 from Bradman. Intriguingly, England fast bowler Harold Larwood insisted that he had Bradman caught behind before he had even opened

Richard Mulvaney of the Bradman Foundation displays Sir Donald Bradman roses in front of Robert Hannaford statue of The Don in the gardens outside Adelaide Oval.

Who's to know what might have been had video replays and other technology been around . . .

his account in the Headingley Test. Who's to know what might have been had video replays and other technology been around in Bradman's day?

One thing was for sure: Bradman's batting was such that his team-mates were constantly overshadowed. With such a good eye, Bradman was able to consistently hit the ball along the ground and find gaps in the field. His driving, especially through the covers, was a sight to behold, while his ability to hook, pull and cut was also second to none. Bradman rarely hit sixes, as he didn't often play risky strokes; he simply didn't need to. Indeed, his highest first-class score comprised 49 fours and no

As chairman of selectors, Bradman chats with Australian skipper Richie Benaud during the historic tied Test involving Australia and the West Indies at the Gabba in December 1960.

sixes, while his highest Test score yielded 46 fours and no sixes. Bradman's first triple ton for New South Wales also contained no sixes, and neither did his 357 for South Australia against Victoria in 1935-36. As reported by Anton Rippon in *Classic Moments of the Ashes*: 'Good balls and bad balls were all equal prey for the man when he was in that mood – as he so invariably was. A good ball on the off stump, designed to make Bradman give a catch behind, was just as likely to find itself pinging away to the leg boundary.'

As Australia contested the West Indies for the first time in Tests – on Australian soil in 1930-31 – Bradman began slowly and finished with a duck, although he scored 223 and 152 in the third and fourth Tests. Bradman's series figures of 447 runs at 74.50 were slightly shaded by opener Bill Ponsford's 467 runs at 77.83, after Ponsford rattled off successive scores of 92 not out, 183 and 109 in the first three Tests.

In the first Test, Bradman claimed the first of his two Test wickets when he trapped West Indian wicketkeeper Ivan Barrow lbw in a rare bowling stint.

With Australia thrashing South Africa 5-0 the following season, Bradman was virtually unstoppable as his scores were 226, 112, 2, 167 and 299 not out. Bradman was unlucky not to reach a triple century in the fourth Test at Adelaide, as the last batsman was run out. With England adopting the controversial bodyline tactics Down Under in 1932-33, Bradman had his most unproductive series but was still Australia's leading run maker with 396 runs. Having missed the first Test, Bradman was out first ball in the second Test when he hooked a bouncer from Bill Bowes on to the stumps.

Bradman's undefeated 103 in the second innings helped Australia to a series-levelling victory, before he made solid but not big scores during England's victories in the next three Tests. Oddly, Bradman claimed his final Test wicket by bowling champion England batsman Wally Hammond for 85 in the turbulent third Test. In the following Ashes series, on English soil in 1934, Bradman averaged just 26.60 with

a highest score of 36 in the first three Tests as the batting order kept changing. Headingley again saw the best of Bradman when he made 304 in the drawn fourth Test, before making 244 and 77 at the Oval. A 562-run victory sealed Australia's 2-1 triumph.

Work as a stockbroker was a decisive factor in Bradman's switching from New South Wales to South Australia in 1934. He averaged 104.60 in 44 first-class matches for his adopted state after averaging 98.53 in 41 first-class matches for his home state.

Bradman captained Australia in his last five Test series, four of which were against England, with his captaincy record resulting in 15 wins, six draws and only three losses. Impressively, his debut series and the bodyline series were the only times Bradman tasted series defeat. His first two Tests at the helm, however, were a nightmare as Australia was twice crushed at home. The captain scored 38, successive ducks and 82. The remaining three Tests were a resounding triumph, Australia winning the series 3-2 and Bradman scoring 13, 270, 26, 212 and 169.

Three centuries to Bradman netted him 434 runs at 108.50 in

The 1948 Ashes was Bradman's swansong, with Australia winning four and drawing one of the five Tests.

the 1938 Ashes, but he had to settle for a drawn series as England won the final Test by a record margin of an innings and 579 runs. Having survived a stumping chance on 40, England opener Len Hutton bettered Bradman's then-record Test score of 334 by 30 runs in a total of 7-903 declared. Australia's hopes of saving the Test were all but dashed as Jack Fingleton and Bradman were unable to bat. Bradman sustained an ankle injury when he landed on a footmark during a part-time bowling stint.

Australia's next Test was in early 1946 following World War II, with Bradman missing his country's thrashing of New Zealand in a one-off Test due to health issues before returning for the 1946-47 Ashes. Bradman's first two scores were 187 and 234 as his team won the first two Tests by an innings, and not

even a duck in the fourth Test could prevent Bradman from racking up 680 runs at 97.14 in a 3-0 series win. Australia beat India 4-0 the following season, with Bradman's scores being 185, 13, 132, 127 not out, 201 and 57 retired hurt.

The 1948 Ashes was Bradman's swansong, with Australia winning four and drawing one of the five Tests. It was this tour that earned Bradman's team the 'Invincibles' tag. The captain entered the series with 6,488 Test runs at an average of 102.98. In his first three knocks he was caught by Hutton off Alec Bedser, who had once bowled him without scoring in the 1946-47 Ashes. Scores of 138, 0, 38, 89, 7, 30 not out and 33 took his average down to 98.88, but his average was beyond 100 again when he made 173 not out in the last innings of the Headingley Test. Bradman's 299-run second-wicket partnership with Arthur Morris set up a seven-wicket victory as Australia chased 404, giving Bradman 963 Test runs at 192.60 at this venue, with four centuries, including his two triple centuries.

With England skittled for 52 in the first innings at the Oval and

Australia losing its first wicket at 117, it was apparent that Bradman would bat only once in his final Test. England captain Norm Yardley and his team-mates greeted the champion batsman with three cheers, Bradman needing just four runs to reach 7,000 Test runs and a guaranteed average of 100. But after defending his first delivery, Bradman was undone second ball by an Eric Hollies googly that beat the batsman's forward defensive stroke and sent the bails flying. It was destined to be the most famous duck in cricketing history, and if nothing else it proved that Bradman was human while perfection was impossible.

While many batsmen have exceeded Bradman's Test runs tally, it inevitably took them many more Tests to do so, admittedly in eras involving much more international cricket than in Bradman's day. Still, one can only wonder how many Tests Bradman would have played and what his figures would have

been had first-class cricket not been abandoned from 1940-41 to 1945-46 due to World War II.

As for Bradman the person, a broad range of comments about him have engendered a mixture of favourable and unfavourable impressions. For any high achiever in any walk of life, someone is bound to try to chop down the tall poppy. In renowned cricket writer David Frith's personal tribute to Bradman, published in *Allan's Cricket Annual 2001*, there were plenty of interesting observations. Frith remarked that perhaps Bradman's most outstanding quality was humility: 'Most really good cricketers are modest. But here was the top man. He knew well enough where he stood in the history of the game. But his modesty was innate, and I don't believe you can fake humility across a period of 30 years.' Frith also reported that Bradman 'vigorously guarded his privacy and that of his family, and he was always very measured and precise and disciplined in his public

Bradman in 1930.

utterances and in his writings'. Frith said that Bradman 'was no more impervious to criticism than the rest of us. But he was careful never to give his critics the satisfaction of a reaction in public'.

As far as Frith's comment about humility was concerned, there were indeed few if any suggestions that Bradman was arrogant. Bradman's son John was quoted as saying that his father 'remained so astonishingly unimpressed by himself'. Frith wrote that John 'expressed the hope that Sir Don would not be deified but would be seen as a human being, with foibles and the odd flaw'. Roland Perry reported in *Bradman's Best Ashes Teams*: 'Bradman's attempt to become anonymous failed to give him privacy but instead enhanced his aura and made him seem, to many commentators, akin to royalty. Bradman's charm was that apart from exhibiting all the normal niceties at public events, he was always transparently *him*.'

According to *200 Seasons of Australian Cricket*, during India's 1947-48 tour of Australia Indian captain Lala Amarnath said: 'Frequently after a game Bradman has come to tell our players over a cup of tea of faults they had made

in batting, fielding or bowling, and how they can correct them.' Perhaps this suggests Bradman was willing to help these particular opponents rather than criticise them.

There have been suggestions that Bradman was aloof from team-mates, if not shy. Arthur Morris reportedly said of Bradman: 'He was marvellous. If you had a problem, you could go to him and sort it out. I find him relaxed and straightforward.' With regard to religion, however, it was evident that Bradman was at the forefront of factions and feuds in Australian teams of the 1930s. In the 21st century it seems trivial that one's own religious beliefs carried any real importance, but in Bradman's day it evidently caused ample problems. Bradman was a Mason, while Catholics such as Bill O'Reilly and Jack Fingleton have been openly critical of Bradman. Fingleton reportedly believed that Bradman was responsible for his omission from Australia's Test team in its 1934 tour of England; leaks to the media also caused problems between Bradman and Fingleton.

Bradman copped criticism as a cricket administrator following his retirement, but a lot of people benefited from Bradman in some way. He received letters in huge numbers until past his 90th birthday, and it became very time-consuming to produce written replies. Bradman also worked for charity, but he did not maintain a high profile through the media as he was by and large a private person. Perhaps it would have been fitting if Bradman had lived to be 100 years old but alas he died at the age of 92. While some famous people fade into obscurity after they retire, Bradman's legacy seems destined to live on forever. His name will always be remembered prominently among cricketing legends.

Career statistics

	Tests	One-day internationals	First-class matches
Matches	52	-	234
Innings	80	-	338
Not outs	10	-	43
Runs scored	6,996	-	28,067
Batting average	99.94	-	95.14
100s / 50s	29 / 13	-	117 / 69
Top score	334	-	452*
Balls bowled	160	-	2,114
Runs	72	-	1,367
Wickets	2	-	36
Bowling average	36	-	37.97
5 wickets in an innings	-	-	-
10 wickets in a match	-	-	-
Best bowling	1 / 8	-	3 / 35
Catches	32	-	131

On his way to becoming the second-highest run scorer in Test

4

RICKY PONTING

Birth date	19 December 1974
Place of birth	Launceston, Tasmania
Nickname/s	Punter
Playing role	Right-handed middle order batsman

Statistics suggest Ricky Ponting had a wonderful career that few, if any, could match. When he retired he was the equal-second most capped player in Test history (alongside Steve Waugh), the second-highest run scorer of all time and had the most Test wins as captain, while also being the first player to achieve 100 Test victories.

Nevertheless, a number of so-called 'unsuccessful' career moments stood out for all the wrong reasons, although they hardly deserved to overshadow the extent of his successes and achievements.

Ponting achieved 48 wins, 16 losses and 13 draws as Test captain. At home he averaged 56.98 in 92 Tests, compared with an average of 46.40 in 76 Tests abroad. He could be deadly on both the front and the back foot, with cutting, pulling, hooking and driving all being considered signature strokes.

When Ponting was aged four, his grandmother gave him a shirt that read: 'Inside this shirt is an Australian Test cricketer'. In the introduction to *Punter: First Tests of a Champion*, it was remarked that when Ponting was a toddler 'a cricket bat was always within arm's reach – an old battered piece of willow took pride of place by his bed'. From the age of eight, Ponting played a mixture of cricket, golf, AFL and soccer. 'Like many Test cricketers before him, Ricky and a small band of budding young Bradmans

When he retired he was the equal-second most capped player in Test history . . .

contested mock Tests in the local park. Here Ricky honed the skills with bat and ball which would eventually take him to the pinnacle in his chosen sport.'

Aged 10, Ponting made an unconquered half-century in just his second primary school cricket match. Aged 11, Ponting scored four consecutive centuries – three of them undefeated – in a schoolboy's carnival. He was uncertain as to whether he wanted to pursue a career in football or cricket, but an arm injury in a football match at the age of 14 proved to be the end of his football career. Fortunately he recovered well enough so that the injury was not of hindrance to him.

Ponting spent a couple of years at the Australian Cricket Academy, and in November 1992 when still a few weeks shy of his 18th birthday he made his first-class debut: in a Sheffield Shield match at the

Adelaide Oval. He scored 56 and 4 for Tasmania against South Australia, having reached his half-century with three successive fours. He stood out in his seventh match, notching 125 and 69 against New South Wales, and later in the season he scored two centuries against Western Australia at Hobart. Ponting again did well in 1993-94, and then started the 1994-95 season with 119 against Queensland before scoring 211 against Western Australia a few weeks later.

Ponting was almost an automatic selection for the second-string Australian team, called Australia A, in the 1994-95 World Series one-day tournament. Although his biggest score was only 42, he was promoted to the top-rung Australian team soon afterwards and made just 1 on debut before his next two scores were 10 not out and 62. Later in the year he averaged a little below 50 on a tour of England with a Young Australia team that – like Australia A – featured players on the verge of international selection. Upon returning to Australia, Ponting scored two undefeated centuries against a strong-looking Queensland team featuring Craig McDermott,

An attacking shot from Ponting goes awry during Australia's 3-0 drubbing of India on Australian soil in 1999-2000.

Carl Rackemann, Michael Kasprowicz and Allan Border.

Following scores of 99 and 131 not out for Tasmania against the touring Sri Lankans, Ponting was selected in the subsequent Test series when Greg Blewett was dropped after struggling against Pakistan. It gave Ponting the chance to play three Tests alongside childhood hero and fellow Tasmanian David Boon. Ponting arrived at the crease with Australia 3-422 following the dismissal of

Michael Slater for 219, and the soon-to-be 21-year-old replicated England's David Gower in terms of registering a four from the first ball he faced in Tests. However, Gower had played an authoritative pull, whereas Ponting snicked the ball through the slips and survived a difficult chance. Ponting scored an attractive 96 in nearly four hours, but just when a century beckoned he was ruled lbw to a ball that appeared to bounce over the stumps. He made 71 in the next Test, and a couple of

weeks later he recorded his maiden international ton as he notched 123 against Sri Lanka at number four in a one-day match at Melbourne. Soon he was promoted to number three, and in the 1996 World Cup he made a century against the West Indies in a round robin game before scoring 45 in the final, which Australia lost to Sri Lanka.

Later in 1996 Ponting was also chosen at first drop in the Test arena, following Boon's retirement. Ponting made just 14 and 13 in a one-off Test in India, before starting the 1996-97 Test season Down Under with 88 against the West Indies. His next three Test scores yielded just 22 runs, and he was somewhat surprisingly dropped from both the Test and one-day teams. His medium-pace bowling, although rarely used throughout his career, brought him two wickets at an average of four in his first five Tests. He captured his maiden Test wicket without having a run scored off him.

Ponting was recalled during the 1997 Ashes and listed at number six for the fourth Test at Headingley where he registered his maiden Test ton. His 127, coupled with opener Matthew Elliott's 199, helped Australia from 4-50 to 9-501 declared to set up an innings win and series lead. Ponting was steady but not brilliant during the 1997-98 season although he notched his second Test ton, this time against South Africa. He cemented his reputation as an excellent fielder, producing run-outs and great catches.

On the 1998 Indian tour he averaged just 21, having received a terrible lbw decision in the first Test. After averaging 11.75 in the first three Tests of the 1998-99 Ashes, Ponting was dropped again. 'It was the first time anyone could recall him being completely out of touch: he seemed to be walking at the ball before it arrived,' Allan Miller wrote in his 1999 Australian cricket annual. Ponting subsequently served

Ponting subsequently served a three-match suspension in the one-day arena after suffering a bruised eye during an altercation . . .

Ponting drives past the bowler during a Test in the Caribbean.

a three-match suspension in the one-day arena after suffering a bruised eye during an altercation in an off-field incident. 'It became the kick-up-the-behind that made me change my approach to life. I did more growing up in the course of that difficult week than I'd done in the previous five years or more. As life lessons go, it was a positive,' Ponting wrote in his book *At the Close of Play*.

Ponting regained his place before too long and instantly proved a point with a century. During Australia's 1999 tour of the Caribbean, Ponting replaced an injured Blewett for the Bridgetown Test, scoring 104 and 22 in a one-wicket loss before scoring 21 and 21 not out at St John's, where Australia levelled the series to retain the Frank Worrell Trophy. Ponting went on to play several handy if not big innings in Australia's 1999 World Cup glory, which undoubtedly did a lot to erase the disappointment of 1996.

Ponting starred in Sri Lanka in the second half of 1999 with Test scores of 96, 51, 1 and 105 not

Ponting savours leading Australia to World Cup glory in 2007 after doing likewise in 2003 and also being a part of Australia's 1999 World Cup triumph.

out, but the hosts won the series. Australia subsequently embarked on 16 successive Test wins, with Ponting having decidedly mixed results. Against Pakistan he scored three consecutive ducks and followed up with 197. He didn't score a duck in his first 44 Test knocks before receiving a woeful lbw decision at Brisbane, and then he suffered the ignominy of a pair on his home turf. Against India he amassed 375 runs at 125 with two centuries, and soon bagged three consecutive ducks in one-day internationals. Ponting,

nonetheless, remained an integral part of Australia's one-day team with his quick and productive scoring as well as his fielding, although he injured his ankle when fielding and consequently didn't play in Australia's 2000 tour of New Zealand.

Ponting averaged 40.33 in Australia's 5-0 clean-sweep against the West Indies in 2000-01, before having another horrendous tour of India: he scored three ducks, while his other scores were 6 and 11. Interestingly, Ponting was promoted to number three during the 2001

Ashes when Justin Langer was dropped. Ponting failed to reach 20 in the first three Tests, and then in the fourth Test he was nearly caught at third slip before scoring. Perhaps the near miss was a turning point in his career, as he went on to score 144 and then 72 and 62. With Langer back in the team as an opener, Ponting made the number three position his own. When he retired, he had batted in the position 196 times in his Test career and averaged 56.27, compared with an average of 40.22, 31.50, 49.73 and 26 in the following four positions.

Ponting topped 1,000 Test runs in each of the calendar years 2002, 2003, 2005, 2006 and 2008. In season 2001-02 he averaged 52.29 at home, having done better in the 0-all drawn series with New Zealand than he did in the 3-0 whitewash of South Africa. He averaged 77.25 in the follow-up series in South Africa, with his 100 not out in the second Test helping Australia to a four-wicket victory when chasing 331 to seal the series. Ponting scored two tons in four innings as Australia crushed Pakistan, also in 2002, and reached triple figures on two occasions while

averaging 52.13 during Australia's 4-1 Ashes triumph.

Having become captain of Australia's one-day team in 2002, Ponting continued to play a key role in multiple series wins in the short form of the game. He led Australia in its unbeaten World Cup campaign in South Africa in 2003, which was highlighted by an undefeated 140 in a total of 2-359 against India in the decider. Ponting was in deadly form in the Caribbean with Test scores of 117, 42 not out, 206, 45 and 113. Australia led 3-0, then he missed the final Test – which the hosts won unexpectedly after chasing 418. While Matthew Hayden's then world record 380 was the highlight in Australia's 2-0 defeat of Zimbabwe later in 2003, Ponting also excelled with scores of 37, 169 and 53 not out. Against India in Adelaide he scored 242, only to fall for a duck in the second innings as the hosts were on their way to losing after passing 500 in their first innings. Next, in the Boxing Day Test, Ponting's highest Test score of 257 helped the hosts square the series. Ponting considered he was in the best form of his life, having registered 11 Test

centuries in 22 months, but more than 12 months passed before he made his next Test ton.

Ponting assumed the Test captaincy following Steve Waugh's retirement in 2004, beginning with a 3-0 clean-sweep in Sri Lanka. Ponting missed most of Australia's breakthrough series triumph in India due to a broken thumb, and

Ponting in action during a Test against the West Indies.

averaged just 28.80 in the Tests against Sri Lanka and India in 2004; his highest score was 92. Australia won two series against New Zealand and one series against Pakistan in 2004-05, with Ponting contributing 841 runs at 93.44, having struck 207 against the Pakistanis in Sydney.

The first major stain on Ponting's Test record was the 2005 Ashes, when he skippered Australia to its first Ashes series defeat since 1986-87. He remarked in *At the Close of Play*: '… our chief problems were we underrated the value and importance of meticulous preparation and practice. Up against

Ponting's marvellous athleticism in the field proved a huge bonus in one-day cricket as well as Test cricket.

a talented well-drilled adversary, spearheaded by a tremendous all-rounder, "Freddie" Flintoff, at his absolute peak, we suddenly found ourselves in deep trouble.' Nonetheless, it could just as easily have had a vastly different outcome.

After Australia won the first Test, Ponting was widely criticised for choosing to bowl in the second Test, and an injury to Glenn McGrath didn't help. Yet England won by two agonising runs in a result that could have gone either way, when an

Ponting talks with bowler Colin Miller, who dyed his hair a number of times during his 18-Test career.

Australian win would surely have set up another series win for Ponting's team. An outstanding 156 from Ponting helped save the third Test, but in the remainder of the series he averaged just 25.38 as England won 2-1. In the fourth Test, Ponting was fined for an outburst after being run out by a substitute fielder: the Australian skipper had condemned England's use of substitute fielders.

At various stages of his career Ponting was prone to the occasional tantrum, earning fines for his misdemeanours. After scoring 164 to lead Australia to a record one-day total of 4-434, Ponting had the misfortune of having that record instantly eclipsed when hosts South Africa recorded a miraculous one-wicket win. He promptly gave what he later deemed to be the biggest spray he'd ever given his team-mates.

After the 2005 Ashes ordeal there were calls from some quarters to sack Ponting, but he went on to lead Australia to glory in 20 of its next 21 Tests, with one draw. First up was a win against a World XI, with this match being controversially awarded official Test status. On home soil in 2005-06 Ponting rattled up five centuries in six Tests as his team beat South Africa and the West Indies, before scoring two centuries in a 3-0 series win on South African soil. The

At various stages of his career Ponting was prone to the occasional tantrum, earning fines for his misdemeanours.

Sydney Test of 2006 was Ponting's 100th Test, and he marked the occasion with 120 and 143 not out in an eight-wicket victory against the Proteas. Ponting also made a vital 118 not out against Bangladesh at Fatullah, where the hosts threatened to record an historic triumph.

Ponting asserted himself early in the 2006-07 Ashes with 196 in the first innings. In the second Test he made another crucial century, albeit after he was dropped on 35. He averaged 82.29 in the series, and Australia became only the second team – after the first in 1920-21 – to clean-sweep an Ashes series 5-0. The year became even better for Ponting when he led Australia to another undefeated World Cup campaign, with Australia turning the tables from the 1996 decider.

Ponting led his country to a 2-0 Test series win over Sri Lanka in late 2007. Australia then led India 2-0 after as many Tests in a four-match series to again rack up 16 successive Test victories. But as was the case in 2001, India broke the streak while

Ponting struggled with the bat. For not the first time, Indian off-spinner Harbhajan Singh had the better of him. Ponting nonetheless returned to form with 140 in the fourth Test, which was drawn, giving him figures of 408 runs at 45.33 in six Tests at home in 2007-08.

The second Test was notorious for many umpiring mistakes, and allegations that Harbhajan had racially abused Ponting's team-mate Andrew Symonds. The Australians were criticised in many quarters, while Harbhajan escaped lightly upon an appeal after he had originally been suspended. Ponting objected to having his integrity questioned, and while he was by no means the only player involved in unsavoury conduct, a few incidents did not cast him in favourable light.

After he was fortunate not to be ruled caught behind for 17, he reacted unhappily when wrongly adjudged lbw for 55 on day one. On the last day, when Australia's Michael Clarke claimed a disputed catch, umpire Mark Benson gave India's Sourav Ganguly out after Benson asked Ponting, who pointed to his chest and then raised his index finger as if to make the decision. Also on day five, Ponting unsuccessfully claimed a catch at silly point even though the ball clearly touched the ground as he was in the motion of taking the catch.

After scoring a century and averaging 53.83 in a 2-0 series win in the Caribbean, Ponting was on the wrong end of a 2-0 scoreline in India. He averaged 38, having finally made a Test ton in India, but Australia lost the second and fourth Tests. Ponting was criticised for his tactics, as it appeared he was trying to ensure he wouldn't incur a suspension for slow over rates rather than try to force a victory.

Ponting subsequently averaged 33.33 and led Australia to a 2-0 win at home against New Zealand, but then he became the first Australian skipper to lose a Test series at home in 16 years. He scored 101 and 99 in Melbourne, but also bagged golden ducks in Perth and Sydney. Australia lost the Perth Test after South Africa chased a 414-run target, and then the hosts lost the Melbourne Test by nine wickets after being on top for a while. Ponting's team at least had the satisfaction of winning the dead rubber Test at Sydney. Australia then beat the Proteas 2-1 in South Africa, with Ponting averaging 35 as this

Ponting dives to safety as an outfield throw misses the stumps during a Test match.

series was also decided with a Test to spare.

However, Australia lost the subsequent Ashes series abroad, following several personnel changes after the 2006-07 whitewash. As was the case in 2005, it could so easily have been different. After Ponting scored 150 while three team-mates also notched centuries in the opening Test, Australia came within one wicket of victory and had to settle for a draw. The series was locked at 1-all after Ponting's team won the fourth Test by an innings, and needed only a draw in the fifth Test at the Oval to retain

... he became the first Australian skipper to lose a Test series at home in 16 years.

the Ashes. Australia fell behind the eight ball and later faced a 546-run target in more than two days. An accurate throw from Flintoff ran out Ponting for 66 following a moment's hesitation from the Australian captain, thus ending a 127-run partnership and leaving Australia 3-217, before ultimately losing by

> Ponting subsequently encountered the biggest stain on his career when he became the first player to lose three Ashes series as captain.

197 runs. Having averaged 48.13 in the series, Ponting was in superb form at times but also faltered under pressure on occasion.

Australia returned to its winning ways against the West Indies, Pakistan and New Zealand in 2009-10, with Ponting's only score of note being 209 against Pakistan in his home state after he was dropped on zero. Ponting had to settle for a drawn series against Pakistan in England in 2010, before again being frustrated in India when his team lost 2-0. Ponting himself was unable to produce a big score. Again, it was a case of so near and yet so far, with Australia losing the first Test by one wicket after an lbw appeal was controversially denied and a run-out chance missed on the same delivery during the last wicket partnership. Having become only the second Australian skipper to lose two Ashes series in England (with Billy Murdoch being the

first in the 19th century), Ponting subsequently encountered the biggest stain on his career when he became the first player to lose three Ashes series as captain. He averaged a miserable 16.14 as his team fell to a 2-1 deficit before missing the last Test with a broken finger; England won by an innings for the second successive time.

Ponting stepped down as captain after his team exited the 2011 World Cup in the quarter-finals, and continued playing under Michael Clarke's leadership. With Ponting still unable to crack a big score, Australia won a series in Sri Lanka before salvaging a 1-all draw in South Africa, and then New Zealand salvaged a 1-all drawn series Down Under. Amid suggestions that his international days were limited, Ponting compiled 544 runs at 108.80 in a 4-0 demolition of India at home, highlighted by 221 at Adelaide after his 134 was overshadowed by Clarke's unbeaten 329 at Sydney.

A string of disappointing scores brought an end to Ponting's one-day international career in 2012, and he called time on his Test career as he struggled with the bat. He made just one half-century in six innings while averaging 24.33 in a 2-0 win in the Caribbean, and then his farewell was a home series against South Africa in which he averaged a mere 6.40. The first two Tests were drawn and Ponting had his heart set on winning his final Test, but it was not to be: the Proteas inflicted a thrashing at the same venue where Ponting had made his Test debut 17 years earlier.

Ponting made plenty of runs on the domestic scene in 2012-13, and had the satisfaction of finally being in a Sheffield Shield title victory for Tasmania when the Tigers had the better of a drawn decider against Queensland at Hobart. Ponting was part of beaten Tasmanian teams in the 1994 and 2012 finals, but missed Tasmania's 2007 and 2011 titles due to international commitments.

Career statistics

	Tests	One-day internationals	First-class matches
Matches	168	375	289
Innings	287	365	494
Not outs	29	39	62
Runs scored	13,378	13,704	24,150
Batting average	51.85	42.04	55.90
100s / 50s	41 / 62	30 / 82	82 / 106
Top score	257	164	257
Balls bowled	587	150	1,506
Runs	276	104	813
Wickets	5	3	14
Bowling average	55.20	34.67	58.07
5 wickets in an innings	-	-	-
10 wickets in a match	-	n/a	-
Best bowling	1 / 0	1 / 12	2 / 10
Catches	196	160	309

Allan Border takes the attack to the New Zealand bowling in an innings win at Hobart in 1993-94, his last season in international cricket.

ALLAN BORDER

Birth date	27 July 1955
Place of birth	Cremorne, Sydney, New South Wales
Nickname/s	AB, Captain Grumpy
Playing role	Left-handed middle order batsman, part-time left-arm orthodox spin bowler

Australia's dominance in world cricket in the 1990s and 2000s might not have happened were it not for Allan Border. His contribution to Australian cricket extended far beyond his records (since broken) of most Tests, most innings, most runs, most half-centuries, most catches by a non-wicketkeeper and most matches as captain.

When Australian cricket fell on hard times in the mid-1980s, Border was the mainstay. He was rock solid, and helped his country become competitive before winning became a habit. Australia finished with 32 wins, 22 losses, 38 draws and a tie under his captaincy. Although a number of his successors had better captaincy records on paper, there was little doubt that the likes of Mark Taylor, Steve Waugh and Ricky Ponting inherited a winning culture that Border deserved credit for establishing.

A left-handed middle order batsman, Border was proficient with a range of strokes, including the cut, cover drive and pull. He was a grafter, a battler and a fighter rather than a fluent stroke maker, and was more inclined to work hard for runs over a lengthy period of time than score quickly, although he could hit out if such a situation was needed.

Australia's dominance in world cricket . . . might not have happened were it not for Allan Border.

Without the influence of former England Test cricketer Barry Knight, Border's career – let alone Australian cricket – could have panned out very differently from the way it eventuated. Border played cricket, rugby union and baseball in his junior days at Mosman in New South Wales, with baseball being his first preference, but by his own admission he had no ambitions with his sport. In his book *Allan Border: An autobiography*, he remarked: 'I played because I enjoyed it and because my mates played. Nothing more than that … The thought of one day playing Test cricket for Australia was as remote to me as being President of the United States. As for captaining Australia … had you mentioned that, I'd have suggested you be certified. Cricket seemed to follow me, rather than

vice versa. I liked the game well enough but, as a teenager, there were too many counter-attractions. In my case, the big one was the beach.'

Border considered ditching cricket to 'concentrate on baseball and chasing girls around the beaches', but he decided to give cricket a real go once he realised that contemporaries such as Andrew Hilditch and John Dyson were making it into Sheffield Shield practice squads. Knight, who captain-coached Mosman and had an indoor cricket centre, took an interest in Border's development and told him he had ample potential, but also effectively implied that he should shape up or ship out, at which point Border decided to shape up. He made his way up the ranks, and was selected for New South Wales in the Sheffield Shield as there were vacancies in the side due to an Australian tour of New Zealand. Border was bamboozled during his debut with Queensland leg-spinner Malcolm Francke causing him plenty of trouble, but scoring 36 felt as good as a hundred for Border in a big win for New South Wales.

The advent of World Series Cricket enabled Border to crack the Test team at the age of 23, in 1978-79.

Border maintained a state berth and also spent some time in England, at Knight's suggestion, before World Series Cricket catapulted Border into international cricket in the traditional format. With a weakened Australian squad trailing 2-0 in the 1978-79 Ashes, Border debuted at the Melbourne Cricket Ground in the third Test and made 29 and 0 in a decisive Australian victory. The hosts squandered a golden chance to equal the series in Sydney, but Border shone with unconquered scores of 60 and 45. He mustered just 11 and 1 at Adelaide as the hosts

Border considered ditching cricket to 'concentrate on baseball and chasing girls around the beaches'. . .

sank to another hefty defeat, but it was something of a shock when he was dropped for the final Test. After being recalled, he was never dropped from the Test team again and played 153 Tests in succession.

Recalled for Australia's two-Test series against Pakistan following the

Border and Geoff Marsh (left) during a tickertape parade after Australia won the 1989 Ashes series 4-0.

host country's landslide 5-1 Ashes defeat, Border made 20, 105, 85 and 66 not out. His maiden Test century had Australia on course for a memorable victory, but after Border was dismissed at 4-305 the hosts astonishingly crashed to 310 all out as a spell of 7-1 from Sarfraz Nawaz – who bowled Border off a deflection – resulted in a 71-run triumph for Pakistan. Border's contributions in the following Test helped Australia to a series-levelling seven-wicket win, as the hosts faced a target of 236.

The next assignment for Border and his Australian team-mates in Test cricket was an Indian tour in late 1979, with the hosts winning the six-match series 2-0. It was the first time India defeated Australia in a Test series, but Border considered it wasn't too bad a result for the tourists considering they had a largely inexperienced team playing in foreign conditions. Border's maiden knock in an overseas Test reaped 162 runs and he followed up with 50 in the second innings, having been reprieved before he had scored in the first innings. The rest of the series was not quite so productive for the left-hander, although he still had respectable figures of 521 runs at 43.42. He also picked up three wickets with his part-time orthodox spin, after previously taking three scalps on Australian soil in his first five Tests.

As the teams returned to full strength following World Series Cricket, Border tallied just 118 runs at 19.67 in a series loss to the West Indies in 1979-80 before averaging nearly 50 in a 3-0 whitewash of England. Against England at Perth, Border erroneously stormed into England's dressing room – out of habit, as he was familiar with being a visitor at the venue in state cricket – and threw a tantrum after being lbw for 4, but he redeemed himself with 115 in the second innings to play a major role in Australia's 138-run victory.

In his first tour of Pakistan, Border was the leading run scorer with 395 runs at 131.67. He made 30 and a defiant 58 not out as Pakistan easily won the first Test, before he failed in the second Test. As the third Test was played on a very flat deck, Border made 150 not out and 153. He also boosted his average when he tallied 77 runs without dismissal in the England-based Centenary Test. Also in 1980, Border made a significant change on the

Border's maiden knock in an overseas Test reaped 162 runs . . .

domestic scene when he accepted an offer from Queensland.

As hosts, Australia beat New Zealand 2-0 and drew India 1-all in 1980-81; Border averaged just 25 against the Kiwis before averaging 45.60 against India. He scored 124 in the third Test against India to help Australia to a 182-run first innings lead, before India recovered to register a famous 59-run win after captain Sunil Gavaskar came within a whisker of forfeiting the match after being unhappy at being adjudged lbw.

While England's Ian Botham gained most of the accolades for England's 3-1 Ashes triumph in 1981, Border was easily the standout batsman with 533 runs at 59.22; Botham was next best, with 399 runs at 36.27. Border's personal achievements, however, were overshadowed by bitter disappointment with the way the tourists squandered winnable positions. In the first Test, Border's score of 63 stood out as neither team could tally more than 185 in Australia's four-wicket win, before the next Test was drawn. In the third Test, which England won after following on at Headingley, Border was bowled by Chris Old without scoring while Bob Willis starred for England with 8-43. The tourists collapsed for 111, when needing 130.

At Edgbaston, Border made 40 in Australia's second innings before he was caught by Mike Gatting off John Emburey, and then a spell of 5-1 from Botham sent Australia declining from 4-105 to 121 all out as England won by 29 runs. In the fifth Test, Border nursed a broken finger as he compiled a gritty 123 not out in seven hours, with Australia losing by 103 runs when chasing a virtually impossible 506. As the tourists salvaged a draw in the last Test, Border made a fine double of 106 not out and 84.

Border had a disappointing series in a 2-1 win against Pakistan in late 1981, before regaining form against the West Indies. For not the first time or the last he excelled in an ultimately losing cause, this time with 78 and 126 in the last Test. The tourists won the match, squaring the series and retaining the Frank Worrell Trophy. Border's form tapered off again, and he was under ample pressure as Australia headed into the fourth Test of the 1982-83 Ashes with a 2-0 series lead. He was bowled by Botham for 2 in Australia's first innings, before a heroic 62 not out in the second innings ensured his place was safe. He added 70 runs with Jeff Thomson for the last wicket, only for Thomson to be caught in the slips off Botham as Australia was merely four runs shy of its 292-run target. Border scored 89 and 83 in the final Test, which was drawn. He finally experienced the joy of an Ashes series win, as the Ashes had not been at stake when the ancient rivals squared off in 1979-80.

Two centuries helped Border tally 429 runs at a magnificent average of 85.80 in a 2-0 series defeat of Pakistan in 1983–84, before he gave a standout performance in the Caribbean in 1984. The West Indies nevertheless won the five-match series 3-0, shortly after the retirements of Australia's star trio of Greg Chappell, Dennis Lillee and Rod Marsh. While Border compiled

Border slashes the ball through the off-side during a Test against the West Indies at Sydney in 1988-89. He took 11 wickets in the Test and scored a painstaking 75 and 16 not out.

521 runs at 74.43, Australia's next best batsman was Wayne Phillips with 258 runs at 25.80. As Australia drew the second Test at Port-of-Spain, Border stoically made unbeaten scores of 98 and 100, lasting a total of 634 minutes. Border scored 98 in a total of 262 before Australia lost by an innings at St John's, and at Sabina Park he notched 41 and 60 not out in totals of 199 and 160 as the tourists lost by 10 wickets.

While Kepler Wessels was the only Australian player to have decent batting figures in a home series against the West Indies in 1984-85, the series was significant for Border as he took on the captaincy. Kim Hughes resigned after Australia lost the opening two Tests, and then Australia also lost Border's first Test in charge before drawing the next one. Nonetheless, Border had something to savour from the series as he scored 69 in the Sydney Test, which the hosts won by an innings to salvage a 3-1 loss. Border reportedly rated Malcolm Marshall as the toughest bowler he ever faced, while Marshall 'loathed bowling to AB and found him the most difficult opponent he confronted' (Hayden, *Standing My Ground*, p. 145).

Border wrote in his autobiography that he was apprehensive at first with regard to the captaincy, and didn't think people would respond to him as they should respond to a leader. Australian cricket was going through some tough times amid a rebuilding phase, while there was also a rebel tour to South Africa taking place. Australia was, however, on level terms after four Tests of the 1985 Ashes series. Border's double of 196 and 41 not out helped the tourists to a series-levelling four-wicket victory at Lord's, before his 146 not out helped secure a draw in the fourth Test at Old Trafford. Border averaged 66.33 in the series, but the last two Tests were forgettable from Australia's perspective as England romped to innings victories.

Australia also lost by an innings in the first Test of the 1985-86

Border wrote in his autobiography that he was apprehensive at first with regard to the captaincy . . .

A turning point in . . .
Border's career was
winning the World Cup
in the subcontinent in
late 1987.

season Down Under, despite Border scoring 152 not out while fellow left-hander Greg Matthews made 115 in the second innings against New Zealand. Australia levelled the series before Border's second innings score of 83 in the deciding Test wasn't enough to prevent New Zealand recording its first series win against its Trans-Tasman rival. As Australia narrowly escaped with a 0-all drawn series against India, Border's best contribution was 163 at Melbourne where rain, following – and coupled with – Border's lengthy knock, foiled the tourists. In a follow-up tour of New Zealand, Border made 140 and 114 not out in the second drawn Test, with Australia showing some promising signs. But the tourists crashed abysmally, with Border failing twice in the final Test as the Kiwis won another series.

Border threatened to quit as Australian captain when the Kiwis forged to a series lead in the one-day internationals, but he chose to stay on after his team squared the series. Australia failed to win a Test in 1986, although the tour of India featured a tied Test in which Border made 106 and 27. Border was dejected to lose another Ashes series as captain, this time at home, although he averaged more than 50 and scored two centuries. He at least relished Australia winning the Test in January 1987 to ensure a 2-1 series defeat.

A turning point in both Australian cricket and Border's career was winning the World Cup in the subcontinent in late 1987. Perhaps Border's most memorable contribution was in the decider against England, as Gatting departed after trying to reverse sweep Border's first delivery before Border's team triumphed by seven runs. Border led Australia to numerous series victories in a range of limited overs tournaments until his retirement, and he played many vital knocks along with also being a fine fielder. While he was a fine catcher in the slips cordon during first-class matches, he was dangerous at cover and mid wicket in limited overs matches and showed an ability to produce run-outs.

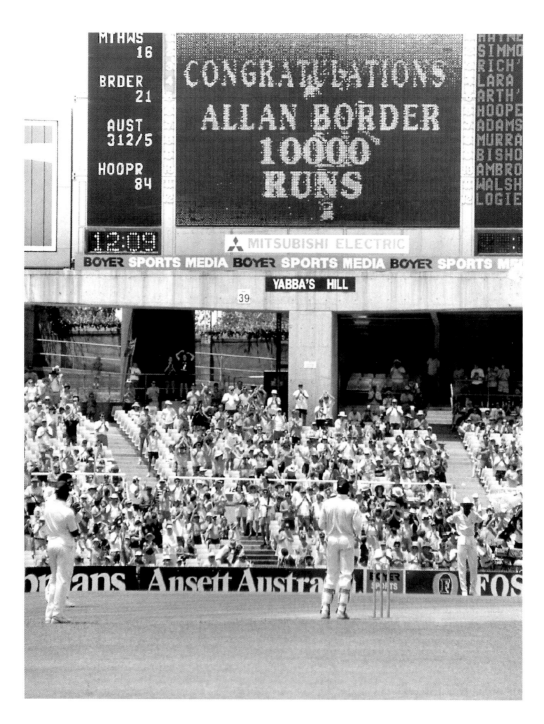

3 January 1993: the Sydney Cricket Ground scoreboard pays tribute to Border reaching 10,000 Test runs. Border made 74 in a high-scoring draw that featured West Indian Brian Lara turning his maiden Test ton into a score of 277.

Following the World Cup triumph, Border finally led Australia to a Test series win. He made his best Test and first-class score of 205 against New Zealand in the second Test, before Australia hung on to draw the final Test. However, the Kiwis were unfortunate to have an lbw appeal rejected when one wicket was needed for them to win the final Test and square the series. Australia lost 1-0 in Pakistan in late 1988, with Border scoring an undefeated 113 in the second Test after being furious with the pitch preparation and standard of umpiring in the first Test, which the hosts won by an innings. Astonishingly, it wasn't until nearly four years later that Border scored his next Test ton.

The West Indies thrashed the Australians 3-1 Down Under in 1988-89, with Border making his 100th Test appearance in the third Test. He failed with 0 and 20 (which came from 111 balls) as Australia fell to a 3-0 deficit, but in the next Test he nabbed 7-46 and 4-50, with Australia winning by seven wickets at Sydney. He scored 75 off a painstaking 330 balls, having been lucky to survive an appeal for a catch when yet to score, and in the second innings he was unbeaten on 16. This Test was the first of a succession of 14 in which Australia did not lose.

The 1989 Ashes was another major turning point for Border and Australian cricket, as the tourists demolished the hosts 4-0, while the other two Tests were interrupted by rain as Australia was on top. With Mark Taylor and Steve Waugh coming of age as Test batsmen and Terry Alderman bowling outstandingly, Border captained the team with aplomb and also compiled 442 runs at 73.67. Without making big scores, Border led Australia to series wins against Sri Lanka and Pakistan in 1989-90, before Australia lost a one-off Test in the New Zealand capital. Border again performed solidly while leading his country to a 3-0 Ashes triumph at home in 1990-91, but the ensuing tour of the Caribbean proved tough. Border captured a five-wicket haul in the second Test but couldn't convert starts into big scores when he batted, and Australia's only success was in the final Test after the hosts had won the series.

Border averaged 55 and led Australia to a 4-0 drubbing of India in 1991-92 but failed miserably in the ensuing World Cup, averaging

Border clips the ball through the legside during a first-class match for Queensland at the Gabba.

just 8.57. Co-hosts Australia missed the semi-finals. Australia's tour of Sri Lanka later in the year featured a memorable come-from-behind win at Colombo, with Border holding a match-turning brilliant catch. He was also made to look like a genius as captain when spinners Greg Matthews and Shane Warne ripped through Sri Lanka's middle and lower order. Australia drew the remaining two Tests, with Border breaking his century drought when he made a crucial double of 106 and 78 in the final Test.

Unfortunately for Border, a series win against the West Indies proved elusive. His last chance was in 1992-93, with Australia leading 1-0 with two Tests remaining and coming agonisingly close to grabbing an insurmountable 2-0 lead. Border made a ton in Australia's victory at Melbourne, after the visitors narrowly escaped with a draw at Brisbane before the Sydney Test was also drawn. As Australia agonisingly lost the Adelaide Test by a single run when Craig McDermott was dubiously ruled caught behind, Border angrily threw his 'worry ball' on to the dressing room floor. The deciding Perth Test proved a nightmare for Border as he made a pair of ducks, including a golden duck in the first innings. In the

The 38-year-old Border scored an unbeaten double century at Headingley during the 1993 Ashes series.

ensuing tour of New Zealand, Border overtook Gavaskar as Test cricket's leading run scorer, and Australia was on its way to an innings victory in the opening Test. But a Kiwi victory in the third and final Test enabled New Zealand to retain the Trans-Tasman Trophy. Border was unlucky to be ruled caught behind for a duck in the final Test when he missed the ball, which skimmed the off stump but didn't dislodge a bail.

Good times returned for Border as Australia won his final Ashes series 4-1, although England won the final Test. Warne's rise to stardom was memorable in this series, with a knock of 200 not out from Border at Headingley being somewhat forgotten. Border's 27th and final Test ton came during a 2-0 drubbing of New Zealand on Australian soil in late 1993, before South Africa toured Australia for

Unfortunately for Border, a series win against the West Indies proved elusive.

Tests for the first time in 30 years. Border must have had flashbacks to the 1981 Ashes as Australia had a big first innings lead and then capitulated for 111 when chasing just 117 in the Sydney Test. Border erred as he shouldered arms to a delivery that removed his off bail in the first over of the final day, leaving his team 5-63.

Border made 84 and 4 in the Adelaide Test as his team drew the series, while there was speculation that the 39-year-old Border could be playing his final Test at home. Border subsequently led Australia on its first cricket tour of South Africa since 1969-70, with the 1994 tour turning out to be his farewell from international cricket. The circumstances were far from ideal, as he felt that the Australian Cricket Board forced his hand to make the decision.

The Africans won the first Test before Australia won the second, with Border making scores of 34, 14 and 45. His last Test was a bore as South Africa crawled to a 153-run first innings lead after batting for 205.2 overs, seemingly content with a drawn series. After making 17 in the first innings, Border made a defiant 42 not out off 166 balls in 225 minutes; Mark Waugh made an unbeaten 113 to guarantee a draw.

Border's career was far from over. He played a major role in Queensland's Sheffield Shield title in 1994-95, including a knock of 98 in the final at Brisbane. It was the first time Queensland had won the title since entering the competition in 1926-27, with Border having played in unsuccessful deciders for Queensland in 1985, 1988 and 1990 while missing a few other deciders due to international commitments. He played on in 1995-96 and averaged a little over 40 as Queensland was unable to defend its Shield title, although Queensland won the one-day final with Border as captain. As Border witnessed Australia regain the Frank Worrell Trophy in the Caribbean in 1995 he was undoubtedly made to feel a part of it, particularly as nearly everyone in the Australian squad had been a former team-mate of his.

Changes in Border's personality were notable over the years, with England players in particular commenting on it. Border came under fire from some critics for having a friendly rapport with 'the enemy' in 1985, before becoming a lot more ruthless, hard-nosed and aggressive four years later. As Botham remarked in *Botham's Century*: 'Border attracted strong criticism for the way he allowed his team to indulge in verbal assaults on opposing players. True, he was responsible for taking sledging to a new level; using it as a systematic intimidatory weapon with which to undermine an opponent's confidence. But his attitude was that mental toughness was as much a part of the modern game as the technical skills of batting, bowling and fielding. He reasoned that if a guy couldn't take it, he shouldn't be out there.'

In his 1986 autobiography, Border wrote with regard to becoming Australian captain: 'I'm never terribly forceful or overbearing about anything. It's not my nature. Don't confuse this with lack of determination. I like to think

. . . he was responsible for taking sledging to a new level . . .

I can grit the teeth just as hard as the next bloke. But a leader of men? I couldn't say.' Nearly 30 years later in his book *Cricket as I see it*, Border remarked: 'I wasn't a natural captain and I'm not a natural leader. I had to learn as I went.'

Border certainly seemed to become tougher rather than mellower as his career progressed, earning the nickname 'Captain Grumpy'. As if the difference in his approach in the 1989 Ashes wasn't enough of a contrast from 1985, he could also be tough on his own players. In the 1986 tied Test, Dean Jones vomited several times and wanted to leave the field as he was on his way to a memorable double century. Border famously goaded Jones by telling the Victorian that a Queenslander was in next, prompting Jones to feel insulted and consequently want to soldier on. On a tour match in England in 1993, Border swore at a struggling and defiant McDermott and said something like: 'Do that again and you'll be on the next plane home.'

Matthew Hayden, who played with Border at state and international level – although only once in the Test arena – remarked in *Standing My Ground*: 'The gloomy mid-1980s had taken their toll on AB – he was a hard man shaped by hard times. You only had to watch a game of cricket with him to see that. He could never relax. He was a big fingernail chewer and had an ever-present worry ball, tossing it from one hand to the other as he poured out his litany of concerns over what was happening in the middle.' Hayden also remarked that Border could be intimidating and his temper was legendary. After Australia lost the first Test in his final series, a livid Border felt that the Australian players were caught up in their 'own

. . . Border could be intimidating and his temper was legendary.

importance on a tour during which we were treated like rock stars, and there was an element of truth to that', Hayden reported.

Perhaps the last word about Border should go to Mark Taylor, who debuted in the Test in which Border claimed 11 wickets against the West Indies, before Taylor succeeded Border as skipper several years later. In *Taylor Made*, Taylor recalled that there was a very good feeling all-round despite Australia being 3-0 down: 'There weren't too many blokes with their heads down. I credit that to our skipper Allan Border,' Taylor remarked.

Career statistics

	Tests	One-day internationals	First-class matches
Matches	156	273	385
Innings	265	252	625
Not outs	44	39	97
Runs scored	11,174	6,524	27, 131
Batting average	50.56	30.63	51.38
100s / 50s	27 / 63	3 / 39	70 / 142
Top score	205	127*	205
Balls bowled	4,009	2,661	9,750
Runs	1,525	2.071	4,161
Wickets	39	73	106
Bowling average	39.10	28.37	39.25
5 wickets in an innings	2	-	3
10 wickets in a match	1	n/a	1
Best bowling	7/46 (11/96)	3 / 20	7 / 46
Catches	156	127	379

Steve Waugh is chaired off the field by Matthew Hayden and Justin Langer as he bows out from international cricket at the completion of the drawn series with India in 2003-04.

6

STEVE WAUGH

Birth date	2 June 1965
Place of birth	Canterbury, Sydney
Nickname/s	Tugga
Playing role	Right-handed middle order batsman, right-arm medium bowler

When he pulled up stumps in early 2004, Steve Waugh was the most capped Test cricketer, before Sachin Tendulkar became the first player to pass Waugh's then record of 168 appearances. Waugh's career figures made stellar reading after he had played during a lengthy period of Australian dominance, yet like Allan Border he had his share of troughs as well as peaks.

Australia did not win any of the first 12 Tests that Waugh played, and he did not score a Test century until his 27th appearance. He was also forced to spend more than a year out of the Test team while his twin brother Mark established himself in the team. It is also astonishing to think that Steve Waugh's first one-day international century was in his 187th appearance. Later in his career he played in 15 successive Test wins (missing one during a 16-game winning sequence), and his captaincy record at Test level yielded 41 wins, nine losses and just seven draws. Steve Waugh was also a two-time World Cup winner.

The elder of the twins by just a few minutes, Steve Waugh was a fiercely determined cricketer who typified mental toughness. His twin was arguably more talented, but Mark's record didn't necessarily do justice to his talent. According to cricket author Allan Miller, Mark Waugh was 'among the most talented batsmen ever to represent his country, yet one cannot escape the feeling that he could have achieved more in his busy career,

Steve Waugh was a fiercely determined cricketer who typified mental toughness.

given a grain more determination. Perhaps that is not his style.'

In his autobiography *Out of My Comfort Zone*, Steve Waugh said he and Mark grew up in the same bedroom for 16 years and 'were in many ways like Siamese twins … A positive was that we always had each other to rely upon … Mark and I certainly had our times of conflict. These increased as we began to clearly exhibit our cricket, soccer and tennis abilities, and, to a lesser extent, in our scholastic endeavours … Sport was our life. Every waking hour was spent playing, watching and discussing anything that had a ball in it. Our first foray into competitive sport came via tee-ball.'

Cricket remained their first love, although their first official game of cricket was something of a nightmare as the twins were bowled without scoring. Playing for the Panania-East Hills under-10s, Mark was out first ball and Steve second ball, with the team's miserly total of four runs including three wides.

'But it wasn't the pair of ducks or the pitiful total that hurt us the most – it was the embarrassment of wearing our only pad on the wrong leg and the placement (by our parents) of our protectors on our kneecaps,' Steve Waugh wrote. The twins nonetheless began to dominate junior representative cricket, prompting debate as to which twin was better. The twins ultimately chose cricket as their main focus after earning representative honours in cricket, soccer and tennis. Steve made the Australian under-19 cricket team, and progressed towards state cricket through playing grade cricket for Bankstown.

Steve Waugh made his first-class debut for New South Wales in December 1984, aged 19, scoring 31 at number nine and having bowling figures of 23-12-34-0 in a draw with Queensland at Brisbane. He flicked a six off impending Test debutant Craig McDermott, and would have had a wicket had Greg Matthews not spilled a straightforward catch. In the Sheffield Shield final at the Sydney Cricket Ground a few months later, Waugh scored a vital 71 at number eight in New South Wales' first innings to help trim

Waugh plays a back-foot drive during a Sheffield Shield match at the Gabba in late 1988 (left) and prepares to fire down one of his medium-pacers in the drawn Bicentennial Test against England at Sydney in early 1988 (right).

Queensland's first innings lead to 56, before the hosts won a cliff hanger by one wicket. 'During this game, the pressure had seemed to invigorate me and I'd played with a clear mind and just let it happen,' Waugh remarked in *Out of My Comfort Zone*. Australian and Queensland captain Allan Border shook Waugh's hand and said 'well played' following his dismissal.

'For him to stop and congratulate me was a significant moment. He was a hero to me and a role model for all aspiring cricketers. I felt a foot taller and my confidence level doubled in that very instant,' Waugh commented in his autobiography.

Steve Waugh began the 1985-86 season with an innings of 107 against Tasmania at Hobart, while his twin made 13 and 28 as an

Waugh is mobbed by Australian fans after reaching his double century against the West Indies at Kingston in the deciding Test of the Frank Worrell Trophy in 1995.

opener in his first-class debut. Mark Waugh's opening partner Mark Taylor made 12 and 56 not out, as he was also new to first-class cricket, and two months later the younger of the Waugh twins was dropped from the New South Wales side while the elder twin was promoted to the Test team. Following series losses to the West Indies, England and New Zealand, Australia sought to rebuild as Steve Waugh, Geoff Marsh and

Bruce Reid were introduced to Test cricket. A young McDermott was still raw and erratic, but sometimes brilliant. Australia narrowly escaped defeat in Waugh's first two Tests, in which his scores were just 13, 5, 8 and 0 as he struggled against spinners Ravi Shastri, Shivlal Yadav and Laxman Sivaramakrishnan.

Waugh had some success with his medium-pace bowling, however, as he had two batsmen caught behind while conceding 36 runs in 11 overs on debut. It was a similar story in Australia's subsequent tour of New Zealand, where he captured five wickets at 16.60 and tallied just 87 runs at 17.40. Waugh scored 74 in Australia's first innings at Christchurch, but the ensuing Test at Auckland was a nightmare for the tourists as they crashed to an eight-wicket defeat, Waugh succumbing to off-spinner John Bracewell for 1 and 0.

Australia's selectors persevered with Waugh. From the time of his Test debut on Boxing Day in 1985, he represented the country in 125 successive international matches (38 Tests and 87 one-dayers) before briefly losing his place in the one-day team in 1990 following poor form. His batting was the reason for his selection, although his bowling was more than handy.

After scoring 59 runs for once out and claiming just two wickets in a drawn series in India in 1986, Waugh showed some promising signs in Australia's 2-1 Ashes defeat Down Under in 1986-87. He averaged 44.29 with the bat, having made three scores in the 70s, and his 10 wickets at 33.60 included five wickets in an innings. Australia's win in the dead rubber fifth Test was its first victory in Tests for more than a year, and was also a first for several of the players, including Waugh. In Australia's World Cup triumph later in 1987, Waugh played some useful knocks but made more of an impact with the ball. Clever bowling in the closing stages helped Australia win some tight matches, including the decider against England. Waugh did enough to keep his Test place without doing anything notable in a subsequent home series against New Zealand, tasting a Test series victory for the first time. But as Waugh conceded in *Out of My Comfort Zone*, the Kiwis were robbed after they were denied an lbw that was 'as "plumb" as there ever was in the history of cricket' when needing

Waugh subsequently showed elements of a great Test cricketer during a series loss to the West Indies on Australian soil.

one wicket in the final Test to square the series.

Waugh had an unhappy time on the Pakistani tour in late 1988, as he was on the wrong end of some dubious decisions, and was also dismissed from a long hop. Waugh subsequently showed elements of a great Test cricketer during a series loss to the West Indies on Australian soil. His scores included 91, 90 and 55 not out, and although his 10 wickets came at a cost of 47.20, he captured 3-77 and 5-92 in the Boxing Day Test. He was also brazen enough to bowl three consecutive bouncers at Viv Richards in the first Test at Brisbane.

The 1989 Ashes series was a revelation in Waugh's career, as he notched 506 runs at 126.50 but captured only two wickets due to back troubles affecting his bowling. In the opening Test, Waugh finally recorded his maiden Test ton. He edged his first delivery but it landed short of second slip, and he went from 10 to 14 as a regulation defensive prod went all the way to the long-off boundary. He amassed 177 not out following his scratchy start, and was again unbeaten in the second Test with scores of 152 and 21. When he was bowled in the third Test to give debutant Angus Fraser his maiden Test scalp, Waugh had recorded 393 runs in 13 hours and 10 minutes at that stage of the series. He lasted 203 minutes for his 92 in the fourth Test and could hardly be faulted for failing with 0 and 14 in his next two knocks.

Waugh averaged 89 against Sri Lanka in 1989-90 following an undefeated century, but he averaged just 11 against a strong Pakistan line-up featuring Imran Khan, Wasim Akram and Waqar Younis, and Waugh also failed to fire against New Zealand. In *Out of My Comfort Zone,* Waugh wrote: 'Maybe it was the fact that I was in commanding form against the lesser-quality attacks that started the dominos tumbling that would eventually lead to me losing my place in the side. I was given a somewhat false snapshot of where I was at and how good I was.

Twins Steve and Mark Waugh cherish Australia's Frank Worrell Trophy win in the Caribbean in 1995. Steve made 200 and Mark 126 in the deciding fourth Test, and shared a match-turning 231-run fourth wicket partnership in Australia's innings win.

'At this stage of my career I was a very good player of average bowling and an average player of very good bowling. The wake-up call Wasim, Waqar and Imran gave me was another part of my overall cricket education, which had to be learnt and earnt before I could consider myself the finished product.'

In the 1990-91 Ashes, Waugh was dropped following scores of 1, 19, 48 and 14. Between the first two Tests the Waugh twins put on a phenomenal unbroken 464-run partnership in a Sheffield Shield match at Perth, Mark scoring 229 and Steve 216: their highest first-class scores. Just two weeks later, Mark made 138 and 23 in his Test debut after being chosen at Steve's expense. Recalled during the 1991 Caribbean tour, Steve Waugh was dropped again following scores of 26, 2 and 4 not out, and 35 wicketless overs.

Cricinfo writer Greg Baum deemed that Steve Waugh's sacking in favour of his younger twin 'was his catharsis. Upon his recall, he minimalised his batsmanship, forgoing risk and waiting for the loose ball, which he still punished severely'. As Allan Border reported in *Cricket as I see it*: 'He came into the side in 1985 when we were struggling, and was a thrashing machine who would play big shots to almost every ball. He had no defensive instinct at all, but through his own skill acquisition he became the complete player over time.'

Waugh remained in Australia's one-day team and was often more effective with the ball in this form of the game in 1991-92. Recalled for Test cricket following 19 months on the outer, Waugh was promoted to number three and averaged just 25.33 against the West Indies despite one century. However, in England he regained his touch when batting at number six, and from that point on he was used at five or six. Waugh averaged 83.20 in the 1993 Ashes with a best score of 157 not out at Headingley – the scene of his first Test ton – where he added 332 runs with Border before the captain declared at 4-653.

Waugh made a ton and averaged 216 for once out against New Zealand in 1993-94, but hamstring troubles forced him to miss the first two Tests against the Proteas. In the

third Test, Waugh made 164 and 1 while also capturing 4-26 and 0-4 to set up a 191-run victory to square the series. In the follow-up tour of South Africa, Waugh again helped Australia level the series. This time he made 86 and then captured his best Test figures of 5-28 to set up a nine-wicket triumph at Cape Town, where he also produced a vital run-out. Later in the year he scored 98 at Rawalpindi, but Australia could not recover from a 1-0 deficit against Pakistan. Waugh missed the third and final Test due to a shoulder injury.

Steve Waugh averaged 49.29 in the 1994-95 Ashes, and was desperately unlucky not to register a century after being stranded on 99 not out in the final Test when McDermott was run out as Mark Waugh was used as a runner. The following tour of the Caribbean produced another milestone for the Waugh twins as well as Australian cricket, with Australia winning a Test series against the West Indies for the first time since 1975-76. As Steve Waugh made a gritty 63 not out in a miserable total of 128 in the third Test at Port-of-Spain, he

A triumphant Steve Waugh reaches a century with a boundary from the last ball of the day's play at his beloved Sydney Cricket Ground in the final Ashes Test of 2002-03. This memorable moment overshadowed the remainder of the Test, which Australia lost convincingly after winning the first four Tests.

swore at Curtly Ambrose during an intense 'in your face' one-on-one confrontation. The locals won the match to square the series, then the Waugh duo turned the deciding Test at Kingston in Australia's favour with a 231-run partnership. Mark made 126 and Steve battled his way to his highest Test score of 200, and Australia recorded an innings triumph. There was no way of knowing what might have been had West Indian wicketkeeper Courtney Browne not dropped Steve Waugh on 42.

Having established himself as the world's best batsman alongside West Indian Brian Lara, Steve Waugh continued his great form in 1995-96. He made an undefeated century in the first Test against Pakistan, before missing a Test against Sri Lanka. He then made 131 not out, 170 and 61 not out upon returning. He also claimed 4-34 at Adelaide, with his bowling becoming less frequent but still sometimes proving useful. His fielding also remained consistent even if it didn't earn the attention that his twin's fielding did.

In a one-off Test in India in late 1996, Steve Waugh made a duck and a gutsy 67 not out as Australia

> ... his contributions in the third Test played a pivotal role in Australia winning a fifth straight Ashes series.

tumbled to a seven-wicket defeat. He averaged just 31.33 as Australia retained the Frank Worrell Trophy, having scored 1 and 0 in the final Test after being caught off a long hop in the previous fixture. In South Africa he made a fine 160 in the opening Test, having added 385 with Greg Blewett, who scored 214. In the 1997 Ashes, Waugh averaged a somewhat modest 39 but was still Australia's second-best batsman, and his contributions in the third Test played a pivotal role in Australia winning a fifth straight Ashes series. Waugh ground out a superb double of 108 and 116 in totals of 235 and 8-395 declared at Manchester, as the tourists levelled the series before winning the next two Tests as well.

Waugh averaged 40 without making a Test century in season 1997-98, and in the process achieved the milestone of 100 Test appearances. Waugh also had mixed results with the bat and with the team after becoming captain of the one-day team. He subsequently embarked on another couple of great years from a personal and team perspective. He was one of five century makers in a Test series victory on Pakistani soil in late 1998, before compiling two tons and averaging 83 as he topped the aggregates in another Ashes series win.

Waugh was subsequently appointed Test captain when Mark Taylor retired, and his maiden Test in charge yielded a 312-run win against the West Indies at Port-of-Spain. Waugh scored 100 in the second Test and 199 in the third, but the hosts edged to a series lead before Australia retained the Frank Worrell Trophy after the captain made a vital 72 not out in the first innings of the fourth Test. Waugh bit the bullet and dropped Shane Warne for the fourth Test following lacklustre form from the champion leg-spinner on his return from injury. Warne subsequently returned to top form and Waugh led his country to its 1999 World Cup glory. The captain tallied 398 runs at 79.60 and scored a decisive 120 not out against South Africa to help Australia to the semi-finals.

Waugh made 56 and captained the team superbly in its tied semi-final against South Africa, but he didn't need to bat in the decider as Australia slaughtered Pakistan by eight wickets.

Waugh broke his nose in a fielding mishap at Kandy in September as Australia sank to a series loss against Sri Lanka, before Australia embarked on its winning sequence of 16 Tests. First up was a one-off Test in Zimbabwe, where Waugh made 151 not out in a 10-wicket victory. Waugh averaged just 14.50 against Pakistan before scoring 150 in the first Test against India, and then in New Zealand he again made 151 not out as Australia romped to its third successive 3-0 whitewash. The following summer Australia whitewashed the West Indies 5-0, with Waugh missing the third Test due to injury before registering three figures in each of the last two Tests.

Waugh scored one century in India, averaging 48.60, but Australia went on to lose the second Test after Waugh enforced the follow-on when a 17th successive victory beckoned. Nobody could doubt the merit of his decision, considering his team had a 274-run lead, but

Waugh and West Indian fast bowler Curtly Ambrose exchange stares during a fierce confrontation at Port-of-Spain in 1995. West Indian skipper Richie Richardson arrives to drag Ambrose away.

India levelled the series with a shock 171-run win before scraping home by two wickets in the deciding Test. Waugh compiled 47 in both innings and made a crucial lapse in the first innings, as he was out handled the ball. He scored 105 in the first innings of the 2001 Ashes and finished the series with 157 not out at the Oval. He battled injury during his undefeated ton in the final Test as he helped Australia to a 4-1 series win. Adam Gilchrist deputised as skipper when injury forced Waugh to miss the fourth Test, which England won.

Although nothing could detract from Waugh's outstanding captaincy record, he admittedly played in a very strong team for a number of years. Cricket historian Gideon Haigh reported on *Cricinfo*: 'The

The slog-sweep became one of Waugh's pet shots.

martial air of his name extended to the field, where he was as ruthless and relentless as he was self-effacing off of it … Nor was it just the surname that lent his leadership a martial air. His Tests were frontal assaults, carefully plotted, relentlessly executed.'

Aged 36, the Waugh twins appeared to be on the decline when they were dropped from Australia's one-day team for good following a disappointing 2001-02 season in the limited overs arena. In the Tests, Steve Waugh also struggled with scores of 3, 0, 8 and 67 in a drawn series with the Kiwis, before averaging 35.25 in a 3-0 thumping of the Proteas, with a top score of 90. In the follow-up tour of South Africa, he again disappointed with scores of 32, 0, 14, 7 and 42. Later in 2002 he scored an unconquered century during a 3-0 drubbing of Pakistan, while his twin averaged 20 and was dropped. Mark promptly retired from international cricket and played state cricket until the end of the 2003-04 season.

Steve Waugh found himself under pressure in the 2002-03 Ashes despite Australia winning the first four Tests. He scored 77 in the first innings of the Boxing Day Test, but averaged a sub-par 32.83 in the first four Tests. In the final Test at his beloved Sydney Cricket Ground, Waugh memorably cover drove off-spinner Richard Dawson for four from the last ball of day two to reach 102. Unfortunately for Waugh, he was dismissed the following morning without adding to his score before making just 6 in the second innings as Australia tumbled to a hefty defeat. Such was the adoration that Waugh's last-ball four generated, it was seemingly forgotten that Australia was thrashed and that Waugh was not retiring. His exit from international cricket came

Waugh evidently deemed that the 'baggy green' was sacred, and was very highly regarded by many team-mates and fans.

a year later: also in a January Test at the Sydney Cricket Ground.

The Waugh twins were part of the New South Wales team that won the one-day and first-class competitions in 2003, with Steve ultimately having one more year in him. On the Caribbean tour in 2003, Steve Waugh batted just twice in the first three Tests and scored 25 and 115 as his team romped to a 3-0 lead. In the final Test, Waugh scored 41 and 45 not out before suffering the misfortune of captaining the team that conceded the most runs in the fourth innings to lose a Test, the hosts reaching their 418-run target with three wickets to spare. In July 2003, Waugh made not-out scores of 100 and 156 in Australia's first two Tests against Bangladesh, both of which resulted in innings wins to Waugh's team.

Waugh's final season involved two Tests against Zimbabwe and four against India, with Australia beating

Zimbabwe 2-0 before a 1-all draw enabled India to retain the Border-Gavaskar Trophy. Waugh made 78 and 61 against Zimbabwe, then his scores against India were 0 (as he was out hit wicket), 56 not out, 30, 42, 19, 40 and 80. India topped 700 in Waugh's last Test to all but ensure Australia couldn't win, although the hosts reached 6-357 after being set 443.

Waugh evidently deemed that the 'baggy green' was sacred, and he was very highly regarded by many team-mates and fans. Outside of cricket he was prominently involved in charity work, with the Steve Waugh Foundation helping people up to 25 years of age with rare diseases. Various aspects of Waugh, though, have brought about mixed descriptions. His ruthless demeanour could sometimes come across as arrogance, particularly as Australia was notorious for sledging opponents as well as winning regularly. If he was concerned about playing in the right spirit, it could be argued that the captain could have done more to clamp down on some unsavoury on-field incidents. In *Standing My Ground*, Matthew Hayden said that Waugh 'may come across as tough and to the point – which he is – but he's also sensitive, thoughtful, emotional and shy'.

A very partisan New South Welshman, Waugh was well known among Australian teams for gloating, 'rubbing it in' and ribbing non-New South Wales players in the Australian team when New South Wales won a title. Conversely, he could not seem to handle being on the receiving end of such behaviour all that well when another state, particularly Queensland, won a title. In 2000, when Queensland won the first-class competition while New South Wales finished dead last as the Australian team toured New Zealand, Matthew Hayden and Justin Langer – on behalf of the non-New South Wales players in the Australian team – relished presenting Waugh with a wooden spoon.

After being dropped from the Test side in Australia's 1999 Caribbean tour, Warne seemed to forever hold a grudge against Waugh, describing Waugh as the most selfish cricketer he had ever played alongside. Similarly, Ian Chappell described Steve Waugh as the most selfish Australian cricketer he'd ever seen. Hayden and Langer jumped to Waugh's defence. Commenting to Fox Sports, Langer said Waugh was 'probably one of the most selfless players' Langer ever played alongside. 'The things that he did for people behind the scenes were unbelievable. Certainly personally, and I know a lot of guys who say the same thing. He was a great leader,' Langer said.

'Great leaders make tough decisions. No one's got a God-given right to play for Australia. Sometimes tough calls have to be made. Steve Waugh should be applauded for it … not criticised for it.'

In a column for news.com.au, Hayden remarked: 'Steve was a leader for the "little people" — he instilled confidence and made you believe because he himself believed that anything was possible. Unless I'm a bad judge, I say Steve Waugh takes his place rightly and respectfully as a unique Australian sporting treasure.'

Career statistics

	Tests	One-day internationals	First-class matches
Matches	168	325	356
Innings	260	288	551
Not outs	46	58	88
Runs scored	10,927	7,569	24,052
Batting average	51.06	32.91	51.95
100s / 50s	32 / 50	3 / 45	79 / 97
Top score	200	120*	216*
Balls bowled	7,805	8,883	17,428
Runs	3,445	6,761	8,155
Wickets	92	195	249
Bowling average	37.45	34.67	32.75
5 wickets in an innings	3	-	5
10 wickets in a match	-	n/a	-
Best bowling	5/28 (8/169)	4 / 33	6 / 51
Catches	112	111	273

Adam Gilchrist salutes the Perth crowd in December 2006 after posting a century from just 57 balls in an Ashes Test.

7

ADAM GILCHRIST

Birth date	14 November 1971
Place of birth	Bellingen, New South Wales
Nickname/s	Gilly, Churchy
Playing role	Wicketkeeper-batsman

In more than 100 years of Test cricket,
Adam Gilchrist undoubtedly became the most influential
wicketkeeper-batsman of all time. The yardstick for
the wicketkeeper-batsman role can always be traced
back to Gilchrist, despite all of the years of Test cricket
preceding him.

Until he became established
in the Test arena, it was
par for the course for a team to
have a number seven batsman
who could average 25 to 30 and
be as proficient as possible with
the wicketkeeping gloves. Having
averaged in the high 40s with the
bat, Gilchrist became better known
as a proficient – dominant might be
a better word – batsman while being
a sufficient enough wicketkeeper. A
wicketkeeper being described as an
'all-rounder' was virtually unheard
of until Gilchrist inadvertently
brought about the tag.

Gilchrist played more soccer
than cricket in his early primary

school years at Junee, and received a
complimentary write-up in the local
press when his team lost 9-0. With
a father who was keen on cricket,
Gilchrist grew to love cricket.
After the Gilchrist family moved to
Deniliquin, seam and swing bowler
Terry Alderman became a hero for
young Adam. He enjoyed watching
Alderman bowl in the 1981 Ashes,
and liked to impersonate Alderman
in the backyard.

It didn't take long for Gilchrist
to lose interest in becoming a
bowler. As Gilchrist commented
in *True Colours*, when shopping in
Shepparton at the age of eight or
nine: 'I saw some wicketkeeping

Gilchrist takes a brilliant one-handed catch to account for India's Sourav Ganguly at the Adelaide Oval in December 1999.

gloves, white leather with green rubber on the palms, and I guess it was love at first sight. They were perfect. I couldn't wait to get them on. Santa Claus took the hint and that was it. I became a wicketkeeper for life … With keeping, I loved the involvement in the game. You never got bored. You were involved every single ball. I was really keen on my batting as well.'

After the Gilchrist family moved again, Adam's father Stan built a cricket net in the backyard of the family home in Lismore. Gilchrist reported in *True Colours*: 'Dad became the regional director of coaching on the Far North Coast, so kids would come over to our backyard net for tryouts and skills sessions. For me that was heaven – it meant more cricket … Looking back, Dad's method was way ahead of its time. I don't know if even the Australian team was training as systematically as we were in the mid-

1980s. Dad would draw up batting and keeping routines for me, fitness programs too, including forearm curls using a water bottle as the weight … As a coach, Dad was at the leading edge in recognising how big a part overall physical fitness plays in the game of cricket.'

At the age of 13, Gilchrist was picked for North Coast Zone trials. Soon after turning 14, Gilchrist notched his maiden century as he blasted 168 in a total of 6-236 for Far North Coast against Illawarra.

After breaking into international cricket more than 10 years later, Gilchrist became more renowned as an entertaining left-handed batsman than for his wicketkeeping skills, and few other wicketkeepers could be described as match-winners with the bat. He became the first player to hit 100 sixes in Test cricket, and also became one of just two wicketkeepers to notch 400-plus Test dismissals. His 472 dismissals in one-day internationals were also a record. There were sometimes question marks over his ability to keep wickets against spin, but he became proficient against the leg-spin of Shane Warne and Stuart MacGill while also taking plenty of catches off quick bowlers such as

. . . Gilchrist became more renowned as an entertaining left-handed batsman than for his wicketkeeping skills . . .

Glenn McGrath, Jason Gillespie and Brett Lee.

Gilchrist played no small part in Australia winning 73 of his 96 Tests, while he was on the losing side just 11 times. An intriguing aspect of Gilchrist's career was that he didn't make his Test debut until he was just shy of his 28th birthday. Would he have achieved 500- or 600-plus dismissals and maintained a high batting standard had he been able to start earlier? We'll never know.

Gilchrist made his one-day international debut three years before his Test debut, with injury and a subsequent suspension to Ian Healy allowing Gilchrist the chance to get some one-day internationals under his belt. Gilchrist at this stage was a standard number seven batsman, and by no means a standout performer. Indeed, in his first-class debut season for his home state of New South Wales in season 1992-93, Gilchrist was regularly used as a number three batsman while Phil Emery was the established wicketkeeper. Emery was not replaced until he retired several years later. After failing in his minimal chances as a specialist batsman in 1993-94 Gilchrist headed to Western Australia, where he became a first-choice wicketkeeper-batsman. But the Western Australian fans were hostile towards him at first, as they were unhappy the selectors had chosen him and consequently brought Tim Zoehrer's playing days to an end. Until then, the Western Australian faithful had been unfriendly towards Healy considering they wanted Zoehrer instead of Healy in the Australian team.

Gilchrist was preferred over Healy as Australia's wicketkeeper in 1997-98 when the one-day and Test line-ups involved some key differences. Again there was loud disapproval at Gilchrist replacing a long and established wicketkeeper in a senior team. While his wicketkeeping was sound, Gilchrist did little of note with the bat until he was promoted to open in the World Series finals as Australia contested South Africa. Gilchrist scored 20 in the first final, which Australia lost narrowly, before he won over the Australian faithful in the second final as he scored

100 off 104 balls to set up a seven-wicket victory. It was a sign of things to come in his international career, with Gilchrist becoming one of the cleanest hitters of a cricket ball and keen to score quickly and play aggressively without being cavalier or reckless. He was strong on both the front and the back foot as he played strokes on both sides of the wicket. He was just as good at picking gaps as he was at hitting the ball over the top of fielders.

Gilchrist averaged in the mid 30s with the bat in his 287 one-day internationals, and was a World Cup winner in 1999, 2003 and 2007. In the 1999 final against Pakistan, he slammed 54 off 36 balls to help Australia towards an eight-wicket win after Pakistan succumbed for only 132. In the 2003 final against India, his 57 helped establish a strong start before Ricky Ponting and Damien Martyn helped the total to a match-winning 2-359. In the 2007 decider against Sri Lanka, Gilchrist amassed 149 from just 104 balls in a match reduced to 38 overs per side, with Australia winning comfortably after tallying 4-281. Gilchrist's attacking approach from the outset meant he could be prone to losing his wicket early on, and in a particular one-day

international he slashed a catch to third man off the first ball of the match. On another occasion, he chopped the first ball of a one-dayer on to his stumps as he slashed at a short, wide delivery.

Despite becoming an established opener in limited overs matches, Gilchrist maintained a regular berth at number seven in Test matches yet was as much of a prized scalp for opponents as any of the batsmen above him. If Australia was in a difficult situation with five wickets down, there was every chance that Gilchrist would change the complexion. If Australia was on top, Gilchrist was capable of making the team's position even stronger. His strike rate of 81.95 runs per

. . . Gilchrist did little of note with the bat until he was promoted to open in the World Series finals . . .

100 balls in Test cricket make remarkable reading, if his strike rate of 96.94 in one-day internationals isn't impressive enough.

With ample disapproval surrounding Gilchrist's selection over Healy in Australia's one-day team in 1997-98, there was also some awkwardness when Gilchrist made his Test debut in November 1999. Healy had lost form with the bat and gloves, and reached 395 dismissals

from 119 Tests after playing in the inaugural Australia versus Zimbabwe Test at Harare in October. There was speculation that Healy would be dropped in favour of Gilchrist for the Test series in Australia beginning the following month.

Healy requested to make his farewell in the first Test against Pakistan at his home ground in Brisbane, where he could reach 400 Test dismissals, but the selectors were unfavourable to the idea. Healy promptly retired, and Gilchrist received a mixed reception as he made his Test debut at Healy's home ground. Gilchrist held three catches off Damien Fleming's bowling as Pakistan made 367, before he arrived at the crease with the hosts having stuttered from 0-269 to 5-342. Gilchrist hit five fours in an over off leg-spinner Mushtaq Ahmed, and his innings yielded another five fours as he scored 81 from 88 balls. A yorker from Shoaib Akhtar ended any thoughts of a debut Test ton, but a fine innings nonetheless earned Gilchrist a warm ovation. Gilchrist held two catches off McGrath and took a stumping off Warne in Pakistan's second innings, before Australia won by 10 wickets.

Gilchrist's second Test was one to remember as he strode to the crease with the hosts in trouble at 5-126 after being set a target of 369 at Hobart. Gilchrist had been stumped for 6 in the first innings as Australia lost its last nine wickets for 55 runs, however, he began his second innings confidently. He quickly moved to 45 at stumps, and Australia began the last day at 5-188. After a quiet start, Gilchrist unleashed a typical array of strokes while Justin Langer grafted away. Gilchrist was psyched up when an off drive took him to triple figures, and the two left-handers put on 238 runs before Langer departed for 127 with victory just five runs away. Gilchrist quickly cut a four and slogged a single to finish with 149 not out from just 163 balls, having registered 13 fours and a six.

Gilchrist scored 28 off 26 balls in the next Test, which Australia won by an innings to seal a 3-0 series win,

Gilchrist's second Test was one to remember as he strode to the crease with the hosts in trouble . . .

Gilchrist is buoyed after reaching a century for Western Australia in the 1995-96 Sheffield Shield final at the Adelaide Oval. Gilchrist made 189 not out off just 187 balls, but Western Australia narrowly failed to win the match as a draw was enough for the host team to secure the Shield.

Gilchrist's first 15 Tests incredibly resulted in Australian victories . . .

with a highlight coming in Pakistan's first innings. Gilchrist flung himself high to his left to pull off a spectacular one-handed catch off McGrath's bowling to dismiss Yousuf Youhana. Australia subsequently thrashed India 3-0, with Gilchrist scoring a duck before notching 221 runs in his remaining four innings. He took another excellent one-handed catch down the leg side, this time to his right as the left-handed Sourav Ganguly miscued a hook shot off Fleming.

With Australia completing a 3-0 rout of the Kiwis in New Zealand, still in season 1999-2000, Gilchrist played a crucial role in the final Test: he took five catches in each of New Zealand's innings, mostly off the quick bowlers. England duo Bob Taylor and Robert 'Jack' Russell had been the only previous wicketkeepers to snare 10 dismissals in a Test. Gilchrist's performance with the bat could also not be underestimated as he hit 75 off 80

balls, including 16 fours, to help Australia from 6-104 to 7-223 and ultimately 252 all out in response to New Zealand's 232. Barely nine months after making his Test debut, Gilchrist was named vice-captain when Warne was demoted due to off-field troubles.

Gilchrist's first 15 Tests incredibly resulted in Australian victories, including a 5-0 clean-sweep against the West Indies in 2000-01. Gilchrist captained the hosts in the third Test at Adelaide as Steve Waugh was sidelined. John 'Jack' Blackham and Barry Jarman had been the only previous wicketkeepers to lead Australia in Test cricket. Gilchrist scored 9 and 10 not out, and was at the non-striker's end when the winning runs were hit. In the fifth Test, Gilchrist was dropped first ball at 5-289 in reply to the West Indies' 272, and went on to make 87 to help set up a lead of 180. In the first Test in India, Gilchrist remarkably reached triple figures in just 84 balls after taking 16 balls to open his account. His 122 off 112 balls included 15 fours and four sixes and he also held six catches in the match, which the tourists won by 10 wickets.

Things unravelled when Australia sought its 17th successive

Adam Gilchrist · 117

Gilchrist and his Australian team-mates rejoice after the wicketkeeper catches Sri Lanka's Russel Arnold off Glenn McGrath in the 2007 World Cup final.

Test win as well as a series victory on Indian soil. Gilchrist was desperately unlucky to be ruled lbw for a golden duck as the ball pitched outside leg stump before he edged it on to his pads, then Harbhajan Singh struck again next ball to claim a hat-trick. Australia nonetheless enforced the follow-on after gaining a first innings lead of 274, before V.V.S. Laxman (281) and Rahul Dravid (180) put on a staggering 376-run partnership. Set 384, Australia collapsed for 212, with Gilchrist bagging a king pair after sweeping at Sachin Tendulkar and this time correctly being adjudged lbw. In the final Test, which India won by two wickets, Gilchrist was twice dismissed for 1 as he was adjudged lbw to Harbhajan in both innings.

In his Ashes debut in 2001, Gilchrist struck 20 fours and five sixes in his 152 off 143 balls to help set up an innings victory. Gilchrist averaged 68 in the 4-1 series win. There was a glitch as he captained Australia in the fourth Test, which England won by six wickets after he set a target of 315 from a maximum of 110 overs. In the following Australian summer, Gilchrist slammed a century in the opening Test against New Zealand, before having some sub-standard results that would not have disgraced virtually any other Test wicketkeeper.

In Australia's tour of South Africa in early 2002, Gilchrist recorded his highest Test score as he blazed 204 not out off just 213 balls at Johannesburg, having registered 19 fours and eight sixes. The innings was all the more sensational given that Gilchrist, by his own admission, was in a 'terrible state' when he walked in to bat, with the visitors 5-293 and 10 overs remaining before stumps. He was distressed and upset about malicious rumours that a former team-mate had fathered his baby son, Harry. 'I don't know how I didn't get out to the first ball,' Gilchrist wrote in *True Colours*, noting he was almost in tears after

> . . . Gilchrist, by his own admission, was in a 'terrible state' when he walked in to bat . . .

batting partner Damien Martyn asked him if he was all right. 'We batted on, and I hit the ball in pure anger ... Given the intensity of my emotions, I was lucky to be there at stumps on 25.'

Gilchrist was in a much calmer frame of mind the next day, but upon reaching 100 he cried for the first time on a cricket field. 'By focusing on making a century, and wanting it as something to dedicate to my wife and new son, I had been able to shut out the hurt and anger,' he wrote. Additionally, Gilchrist rated his 317-run partnership with Martyn as on a par with his partnership with Langer in Gilchrist's second Test.

Australia won the Johannesburg Test by an innings and 360 runs – then the second-biggest margin in Test history – before tottering at 5-176 in reply to South Africa's 239 during the Cape Town Test. 'I had such a clear head, it was like a

Gilchrist goes on the attack during a one-day match for his country in early 2008.

mixture of my first Test innings and the day we brought Harry home from hospital – just joy,' Gilchrist wrote, before noting that he made 138 not out from 108 balls. 'It was pure fun. I remember when I made my hundredth run ... looking up and seeing [wife] Mel in the partners' box with other wives and girlfriends. Among them was this tiny little face – Harry. I was laughing my head off.'

Australia won by four wickets, with Gilchrist scoring 24 in Australia's second innings as the tourists sought 331, before he made 91 and 16 in the third Test – which the Proteas won after their opponents appeared set for their sixth successive win against South Africa.

Gilchrist averaged 40.67 in a 3-0 whitewash of Pakistan, and then averaged 55.50 in a 4-1 victory against England. His lone century came in the final Test, which England won, and Gilchrist was the non-striker when Steve Waugh memorably reached a century from the final ball of a day's play. After averaging 70.50 in the Caribbean in 2003 – having scored an undefeated century in the 3-1 series win – and scoring 113 not out and 20 in home Tests against Zimbabwe later that year,

Gilchrist's batting average was 60.25 after 47 Tests. He underwent a form slump against India and Sri Lanka in early 2004, and at one stage made successive scores of 6, 4, 4, 0 and 0. On a pair in a Test at Kandy, Gilchrist was promoted to number three and blasted 144 to help Australia to another 3-0 series triumph.

Australia hosted Sri Lanka for two Tests in mid-2004, and Gilchrist scored 0 and 80 as he captained Australia to its 149-run victory at Darwin before Ponting regained the captaincy in the drawn second Test. Still in 2004, Gilchrist had the honour of leading Australia to its first series win in India since 1969-70. As in 2001, he began with a century in a big win.

Australia was lucky to escape with a draw in the second Test of the 2004 series after Gilchrist uncharacteristically fumbled a catch and a stumping, before Australia won the third Test. India won the fourth Test after Ponting returned, leaving Gilchrist with four wins, a loss and a draw from six Tests as skipper. He also led Australia to 12 wins, four losses and a no-result in one-day internationals.

Gilchrist was in fine fettle as he scored 126, 50, 69, 0 not out,

Gilchrist had the honour of leading Australia to its first series win in India since 1969-70.

48 and 113 in the Tests on home soil in 2004-05. Australia beat New Zealand and Pakistan in the process, although Gilchrist was lucky not to be ruled lbw when in single figures during the opening Test. He followed up with 121, 162 and 60 not out in successive Tests in New Zealand, before joining other Australian strugglers in the 2005 Ashes, particularly against the swinging ball. His highest score was 49 not out as he tallied just 181 runs at 22.63, with England finally winning the Ashes after Australia had held the urn for eight successive series. Gilchrist scored 94 against a World XI in October and was twice dismissed for 44 later in 2005, but he had a bad trot as a sequence of single figure scores lowered his average to below 50 for the first time since his four failures in India in 2001.

Gilchrist began 2006 on a strong note, with his 86 in a win over South Africa taking his average beyond 50, although his average was below 50 thereafter. As he notched just 50 runs at 10 in three Tests on South African soil, it became easy to think Gilchrist was well past his prime and that his previous batting brilliance was now infrequent. It was too easy to forget he had become the benchmark for the role of a wicketkeeper-batsman and that his batting record would always be immensely superior to that of other record-breaking Test wicketkeepers such as Healy, Rod Marsh, Alan Knott and Mark Boucher.

After scoring a decisive 144 in a Test in Bangladesh in April 2006, Gilchrist had mixed results with the bat while relishing a 5-0 clean-sweep of England on Australian soil. He began with a duck in Brisbane and scored 64 at Adelaide, then made another duck in the first innings at Perth. In the second innings at Perth he blasted 102 not out after reaching his ton in just 57 balls. At the time it was the second-fastest Test century, as Viv Richards once reached a Test ton in 56 deliveries. It was Gilchrist's last Test century, and he completed the Ashes rout in style with a score of 62 and nine dismissals at Sydney.

Season 2007-08 was Gilchrist's last in Tests and one-day internationals, with Australia accounting for Sri

Lanka and India in the Tests. After scoring an unconquered 67 in his only innings against Sri Lanka, he scored a disappointing 150 runs at 21.43 against India. He scored just 7 and 1 in the acrimonious Sydney Test, and felt that the end was nigh after dropping two regulation catches and two tough chances.

With Australia leading 2-0, Gilchrist enjoyed a Test victory for the last time. India won the third Test then the fourth Test was drawn, with Gilchrist dropping another catch but also becoming the world record holder for wicketkeeping Test dismissals before Boucher reclaimed the record.

Career statistics

	Tests	One-day internationals	First-class matches
Matches	96	287	190
Innings	137	279	280
Not outs	20	11	46
Runs scored	5,570	9,619	10,334
Batting average	47.61	35.89	44.16
100s / 50s	17 / 26	16 / 55	30 / 43
Top score	204*	172	204*
Balls bowled	-	-	-
Runs	-	-	-
Wickets	-	-	-
Bowling average	-	-	-
5 wickets in an innings	-	-	-
10 wickets in a match	-	n/a	-
Best bowling	-	-	-
Catches/stumpings	379 / 37	417 / 55	756 / 55

Keith Miller sends down a delivery during the 1940s.

8

KEITH MILLER

Birth date	28 November 1919 (died 11 October 2004)
Place of birth	Sunshine, Melbourne, Victoria
Nickname/s	Nugget
Playing role	All-rounder (right-handed batsman, right arm fast bowler)

While Garry Sobers and Jacques Kallis deserve to be considered the best two all-rounders (maybe even the two best players) in Test cricket history, Australia's Keith Miller surely deserves to be rated on the next rung.

Miller was just the second cricketer to achieve the double of 2,000 runs and 100 wickets in Tests, after England's Wilfred Rhodes. Statistically, Miller at least deserves to be rated in the same calibre as the likes of Imran Khan, Ian Botham, Richard Hadlee and Kapil Dev. Nonetheless, as Kersi Meher-Homji reported in *Cricket's Great All-rounders*, statistics 'did not provide a yardstick for his greatness. It was his charisma, his glamour, his Errol Flynn-like persona that appealed to the spectators.'

In his book *David Gower's 50 Greatest Cricketers of All Time*, Gower reported that Miller 'did the things that make cricket most interesting to the masses – bowled fast, hit the ball huge distances, held stunning reflex catches – while also possessing Hollywood looks and an unquenchable sense of fun. Having survived Second World War service as a fighter pilot, he wasn't prepared to take anything too seriously and that only served to imbue his cricket with even more zest.' In *The Illustrated Encyclopedia of World Cricket*, Peter Arnold wrote: 'As a player, he was unpredictable in everything he did, and the public loved him for it … Full of fun and often a practical joker, he had moments of extreme seriousness. And his love of classical

July 1945, Australia's team at Lords. Miller is in the back row, third from the right.

Miller was just the second cricketer to achieve the double of 2,000 runs and 100 wickets in Tests . . .

music contrasted strongly with his fondness of gambling.'

At the age of 18, Miller scored 181 at number five in his first-class debut for Victoria against Tasmania at the Melbourne Cricket Ground in February 1938. He didn't bowl during this match; indeed, he was purely a batsman in his early years. His Sheffield Shield debut was at Adelaide in 1939-40, and although he scored just 4 and 7 he ran out one of his future Australian captains, Don Bradman. Miller scored 108 in his fourth Shield match, also against South Australia.

World War II hindered Miller's cricketing career, as first-class cricket was abandoned from 1940 to 1946. Miller also played AFL,

Miller (centre) with Ray Lindwall and Dennis Lillee in 1986.

having lined up for Brighton for a few years before playing for St Kilda from 1940 to 1942. The following few years were dominated by the war, with Miller serving as a fighter pilot. He had some near misses, and survived a crash landing. The horrors of war must have put life in perspective for Miller, who famously responded to a question about handling pressure on a cricket field with the expression: 'Pressure is having a Messerschmitt up your arse. Playing cricket is not.'

Miller played for the Australian Services team in so-called Victory Tests against England in 1945, notching a couple of centuries and taking wickets as he exerted himself as a pace bowler. In the same year, Miller struck 13 fours and seven sixes in a knock of 185 in

Peter Burness, curator of the Fifty Australians Exhibition at the Australian War Memorial, in front of a detailed description of Miller.

165 minutes for a Dominions team against England at Lord's. It was neither the first nor the last time he hammered some monstrous sixes.

Miller resumed playing AFL for St Kilda in 1946 and also represented Victoria that year, but AFL soon gave way to cricket. Miller made his official Test debut in late March 1946 when Australia played a one-off Test in the New Zealand capital. It was the first time Australia and New Zealand squared off in a Test, and it was over in two days when the Kiwis were skittled for 42 and 54 while Australia made 8-199 in difficult conditions. Miller held a catch early on and didn't get to bowl in New Zealand's first innings, before scoring 30 at number four and then taking 2-6 from six overs. Miller's first victim was Kiwi captain and opening batsman Walter Hadlee, who was bowled; the next scalp was number three Verdun Scott, who was caught behind.

Australia's next task in Test cricket was hosting the 1946-47 Ashes, the home side winning the five-match series 3-0 and Miller being one of many players to strongly contribute. In the first Test at Brisbane, Miller scored 79 at number five as the hosts amassed 645, before he shared the new ball with Ray Lindwall. Interestingly, Lindwall bowled 12 wicketless overs while Miller captured 7-60 from 22 overs on a sticky wicket as England tallied only 141.

These figures remained Miller's best throughout his Test career. Two of his victims were lbw, while another two were bowled and one caught behind. Miller took 2-17 from 11 overs in England's second innings, with the tourists losing by an innings and 332 runs; Miller dismissed openers Len Hutton and Cyril Washbrook for the second time in the match. Hutton was bowled for 7 in the first innings and caught by Sid Barnes first ball in the second innings, while Washbrook scored 6 and 13 and he was caught by Barnes both times. Australia also won the second Test by an innings, with Miller's sole victim being Hutton, who was unusually out hit wicket.

Having only chipped in with wickets following his standout display at Brisbane, Miller was Australia's fourth-highest wicket-taker with 16 scalps at 20.88 while being Australia's fourth-highest run scorer with 384 runs at 76.80. In the drawn fourth Test at Adelaide, Miller notched his maiden Test ton as he made 141 not out. A notable aspect of this innings was Miller hitting a six off the first ball of the fourth day. In the final Test, Miller's unbeaten 34 helped Australia to a five-wicket win; the target was 214.

Miller transferred from Victoria to New South Wales for the 1947-48 season and played out the rest of his domestic cricket career there. He also played for the New South Wales interstate football team in the 1947 Hobart Carnival, meaning he ultimately played for two different states in cricket and football. On the international scene in 1947-48, Miller made handy rather than decisive contributions when Australia thrashed India 4-0. His series figures were 185 runs at 37 and nine wickets at 24.78; Miller and most of his team-mates needed to bat only once in each Test in the five-match series.

Miller was again steady if unspectacular during the Invincibles Ashes tour of 1948, averaging 26.29

Miller in action during his AFL days.

with the bat and 23.15 with the ball. His tour figures were outstanding as he tallied 1,088 runs at 47.30 and 56 wickets at 17.59. Miller scored a duck in his maiden Test innings on England soil, and his next effort was only four runs better before he made 74 in Australia's second innings in the second Test. Seven of his 13 wickets in the series came in Australia's eight-wicket victory in the first Test at Trent Bridge. Having bowled Hutton and Denis Compton and had Jim Laker caught behind while taking 3-38 off 19 overs in England's first innings, Miller took 4-125 from 44 overs in England's second innings as Lindwall was injured. Hutton, Compton and Laker were again among his victims,

> . . . Miller made handy rather than decisive contributions when Australia thrashed India 4-0.

in addition to Washbrook, with Hutton again bowled and Compton this time hit wicket after scoring 184. However, Miller did not bowl as often as what might have been expected in this series; indeed, he did not bowl at all in the second Test at Lord's due to a back injury.

Lindwall and Bill Johnston took 27 wickets apiece in the series, and Ernie Toshack bowled more overs than Miller while taking two fewer wickets. Miller seemingly earned the ire of Bradman in a tour match against Essex when Miller allowed himself to be bowled first ball as the tourists were on their way to tallying 721 runs. An apparent falling out involving Bradman and Miller was considered the reason why Miller bowled a series of bouncers to Bradman in a testimonial match, which supposedly was the subsequent reason for Miller's omission from the 1949-50 tour of South Africa with Bradman as a selector. Miller earned a prompt recall, as Johnston sustained an injury.

Miller was promoted to number three in the batting order, and started with 21 at Johannesburg as openers Arthur Morris and John Moroney failed to score. The tourists, however, topped 400, and then Miller bagged 5-40 as South Africa made just 137 and again failed to reach 200. With the tourists winning the five-match series 4-0, Miller scored 246 runs at 41 and snared 17 scalps at 22.94. He did a little better at home in the 1950-51 Ashes, which Australia won 4-1, scoring 350 runs at 43.75 and taking 17 wickets at 17.71. After a quiet start to the series, he was lowered from number four to number five in the batting order and excelled in the third Test at Sydney, where the hosts won by an innings. After taking 4-37 and holding a splendid catch at slip, Miller made his second Test century as he stroked a cautious and somewhat subdued 145 not out. Miller narrowly missed scoring a ton in the following Test at Adelaide as he was bowled by leg-spinner Doug Wright for 99.

Australia's leading all-rounder had to wait until the following summer to register his third Test ton, which came in the second Test of the home series against the West Indies. Miller's 129 at Sydney helped set up a 2-0 lead, before finishing the series with 362 runs at 40.22 and 20 victims at 19.90. Miller bagged seven scalps in each of the last two Tests, including two five-wicket hauls, with Australia winning 4-1 although not before the West Indies nearly levelled the series in the penultimate Test – the hosts scraped home by one wicket following a last wicket stand of 38.

Miller performed soundly rather than prominently against South Africa in 1952-53, averaging 25.50 with the bat and 18.54 with the ball. He and Lindwall were out due to injury and sorely missed when South Africa won the final Test to draw the series. Miller's figures were modest in the 1953 Ashes, England winning the urn for the first time in 20 years: the all-rounder averaged 24.78 with the bat and 30.30 with the ball as he took just 10 wickets. At Lord's, however, he scored a sparkling 109, possibly his finest Test knock. As the only outright result in the series was in the final Test, which England won by eight wickets at the Oval, Miller failed with 1 and 0 while

Australia's leading all-rounder had to wait until the following summer to register his third Test ton . . .

taking two wickets in 45 overs across England's two innings. Miller also underachieved in the 1954-55 Ashes, with his highest score being 49 while he averaged 23.86 with the bat and took 10 wickets at 24.30.

For not the first time, injury forced him to miss a match that proved crucial in the outcome of a series. Hosts Australia won the opening battle by an innings, but Miller missed the second Test. The visitors won by 38 runs, when a strong batting or bowling contribution from Miller could have tilted the balance Australia's way. There is little point speculating about it and Miller returned for the remainder of the series, which ultimately went England's way 3-1.

Miller did his best to keep Australia in contention. In the third Test at Melbourne he had wonderful figures of 11-8-14-3, having dismissed Hutton and the other opener, Bill Edrich, as well as

Compton. But Miller twice failed with the bat as Australia sank to a 128-run loss, which gave England the series lead. In the following Test at Adelaide, with England needing a mere 94 runs to secure the Ashes, the tourists were in strife at 3-18 after Miller accounted for Hutton, Edrich and Colin Cowdrey. A fine diving catch from Miller induced the dismissal of Peter May, to leave England still shakily placed at 4-49, although England went on to win by five wickets.

Miller peaked as a Test batsman on Australia's 1955 Caribbean tour, tallying 439 runs in six innings, with three centuries. His 147 helped Australia win the first Test, and in the drawn fourth Test he scored 137 and 10. In the final Test, which Australia won by an innings to seal a 3-0 series win, Miller was one of five century makers for the tourists. Miller's bowling was a little below par with 20 wickets at 32.05, but in the final Test he had figures of 6-107 and 2-58 to go with his 109.

As there was no Test cricket on Australian soil in the summer of 1955-56, Miller captured his best first-class figures of 7-12 when New South Wales routed South Australia for just 27. It was one of many domestic highlights for Miller, who captained New South Wales 26 times for 14 wins and just two losses, having taking on the leadership in 1952-53. The 1955-56 season was the third in a row in which New South Wales won the Sheffield Shield, with no other state winning the Shield until 1962-63.

In the 1956 Ashes, Miller was more effective with ball than bat, averaging around 22 in both departments. He took 5-72 and 5-80 at Lord's – surprisingly the only 10-wicket match haul in his first-class career – where he also scored 28 and 30 as the tourists took the series lead with a 185-run drubbing. But as England won the next two Tests by an innings, Miller fell to the wiles of England off-spinner Jim Laker on four consecutive occasions. Laker captured 11 scalps in the third Test and a phenomenal 19 in the fourth Test, after Laker had also dismissed Miller twice in the drawn first Test. In a tour match Miller made his highest first-class score, amassing 281 not out against Leicestershire.

As a knee injury had become troublesome for Miller, he was destined to play just one more Test following the 1956 Ashes. Miller's Test farewell was Australia's first

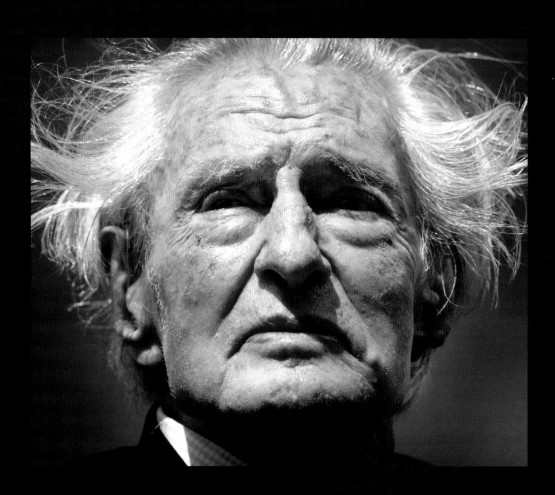

Miller in his latter years.

meeting with Pakistan, on matting at Karachi in October 1956. He top scored with 21 in a miserable total of 80 before taking 2-40 from 17 overs, and then made 11 before taking 0-18 from 12 overs as the hosts won by nine wickets.

Tributes were aplenty following Miller's passing at the age of 84, in October 2004. In *Cricket's Great All-rounders*, Fred Trueman, who was the first player to take 300 Test wickets, said: 'Miller will go down in the history of Test cricket as one of the greatest all-rounders of all time. In my opinion, he will also remain the biggest enigma that Australian cricket ever produced or is likely to. He had the flair, as any cricketer of the highest class must have, to be able to perform great deeds that surpass even one's own expectations. He also had a great personality that influenced all who came into contact with him and I do not think anyone could say they knew how great he would react to a situation on a cricket field. That was where his greatness lay.' In *Wisden Asia Cricket* magazine, David Frith reported in an article about Miller that there had 'never been a more glamorous cricketer than Keith Miller', and

> In the 1956 Ashes, Miller was more effective with ball than bat . . .

concluded with the words: 'The more striking a young man's elan and image, the tougher it must be to endure the privations of the later years. In this, Keith Miller was surely cricket's Dorian Gray.'

Miller's lifestyle choices ensured he got into plenty of mischief and was never far from seedy and sordid situations. Despite this, his marriage to Peg lasted from 1946 until late 2002, then he married Marie Challman in 2004. A two-part *Australian Story* documentary focused first on his stellar cricketing career, then on his personal life. As Spiro Zavos reported: 'The documentary was introduced by Shane Keith Warne, a latter-day Keith Miller in some respects.

'I couldn't help thinking that Miller was lucky in a sense that he did not live as Warne has in the era of celebrity journalism and promotion. Miller's high life would have been the stuff of the tabloids,

Miller's lifestyle choices ensured he got into plenty of mischief and was never far from seedy and sordid situations.

instead of his incisive cricket articles for *The Daily Express* and *The Australian*, which were often written despite the fact that he had not actually bothered attending the match that particular day.

'Having said this, Miller was a far more likeable, sophisticated, well-educated and well-mannered rogue than Warne.

'Miller was a charming man. This is a description that can never be applied to Warne.

'Miller's back story, too, the profound effect his war service in bombers in the Second World War had on his attitude to life, provides a convincing rationale for his determination to live his life as if there was not going to be a tomorrow.'

As reported on www.abc.net.au/austory/the-millers-tale—part-1/9172986, Miller's niece Jan Beames said: 'He's basically had two lives. And I don't think he integrated the two lives. So when he was home with Peg, he was home with Peg and the boys. When he was away or interstate, then he was like a playboy.' Keith Miller's son Bill said of his father: 'Well, he wasn't much of a husband. He was always playing around. I mean, he made Shane Warne look like an altar boy, and he used to do it openly in front of us.'

Miller reportedly fell out with a couple of his four sons, although they were said to have patched things up before Miller's death. Ill health, including a stroke, skin cancer and operations on a broken hip, plagued Miller in his late years. The Victorian government staged a state funeral for Miller, with ABC Radio broadcasting it across the nation.

Career statistics

	Tests	One-day internationals	First-class matches
Matches	55	-	226
Innings	87	-	326
Not outs	7	-	36
Runs scored	2,958	-	14,183
Batting average	36.98	-	48.91
100s / 50s	7 / 13	-	41 / 63
Top score	147	-	281*
Balls bowled	10,461	-	28,405
Runs	3,906	-	11,087
Wickets	170	-	497
Bowling average	22.98	-	22.31
5 wickets in an innings	7	-	16
10 wickets in a match	1	-	1
Best bowling	7/60 (10/152)	-	7/12
Catches	38	-	136

Shane Warne celebrates a wicket at the Melbourne Cricket Ground during the Boxing Day Ashes Test in 1994-95.

SHANE WARNE

Birth date	13 September 1969
Place of birth	Upper Ferntree Gully, Victoria
Nickname/s	Warnie, Hollywood
Playing role	Leg-break bowler

Few cricketers, if any, generated as much attention as did Shane Warne. The second-highest wicket-taker in Test cricket, Warne was well known for many things: not all cricket-related, and many of them casting him in an unsavoury way.

He polarised opinion and was effectively a celebrity as much as a sportsman, yet his cricketing deeds will surely remain forever entrenched among the sport's elite.

Warne was offered a sports scholarship to attend Mentone Grammar in the latter part of his schooling years, and in his teens he bowled both leg-spin and off-spin. In 1987 and 1988 he played several matches for the St Kilda under-19 AFL team, before progressing to reserve grade and then being delisted. He turned his main focus to cricket, and found a vital mentor in the form of Terry Jenner. A leg-spinner who claimed 24 wickets in nine Tests from 1970 to 1975, Jenner proved to be an invaluable influence on Warne. After attending the Australian Cricket Academy, Warne claimed figures of 0-61 from 18 overs and 1-41 from 19 overs for Victoria against Western Australia at St Kilda in his first-class debut in February 1991. It was hardly eye-catching, but with just the one first-class appearance under his belt Warne was chosen in an Australian squad to tour Zimbabwe in September 1991. The squad featured several players on the fringe of international selection, as well as Mark Taylor and Steve Waugh, both of whom would later captain Test teams that included Warne. The rookie leg-spinner claimed 11 scalps at 18.82 in

Warne and wicketkeeper Adam Gilchrist enjoy a wicket during the 1999 World Cup in England.

the two first-class matches on tour, with best figures of 7-49.

For the Sydney Test starting on 2 January 1992, Warne was a shock selection as he had played just seven first-class matches and taken 26 wickets at 24.08. He was 12th man for Victoria only three weeks before his Test debut, and in the lead-up to the Boxing Day Test claimed match figures of 7-56 for an Australian XI against a touring West Indies XI. Many followers were surprised at the sight of the beefy 23-year-old with long blond hair. With Australia batting first, Warne appeared at number 10 and made the same score he did in his first-class debut: 20. It was the first of many times he proved to be a useful batsman for his country.

His bowling, however, suggested either he was not ready for Test cricket or that the step-up from Sheffield Shield to Tests was huge. With opener Ravi Shastri scoring 206 and an 18-year-old Sachin Tendulkar scoring an elegant 148 not out at number six, Warne conceded 150 runs in 45 overs. It could have been a different story had he not fumbled a caught-and-bowled chance that Shastri offered. Warne belatedly dismissed Shastri,

He polarised opinion . . . yet his cricketing deeds will surely remain forever entrenched among the sport's elite.

who holed out to Warne's Victorian team-mate Dean Jones at deep extra cover. Warne conceded 78 runs in 23 overs during the subsequent Adelaide Test, and was on the winning team after the Sydney Test was drawn. Warne was dropped for the final Test, which Australia won to secure a 4-0 series triumph.

As far as Test performances were concerned, the first of three turning points for Warne took place in Colombo in August 1992. Having been pasted for 107 runs in 22 overs in Sri Lanka's first innings, Warne had conceded 335 runs and taken just one wicket in his first two-and-a-half Tests. But with the Sri Lankans 6-145 and needing a further 36 runs to win the Test, which the hosts had controlled for the most part, Australian captain Allan Border took a big risk when he summoned Warne to bowl. After off-spinner Greg Matthews took his seventh

Umpire Steve Randell watches Warne send down a delivery in the early stages of Warne's Test career.

wicket of the match, Sri Lanka's last three batsmen were caught off Warne, who had 3-11 from 5.1 overs as Australia stole a dramatic 16-run victory.

The second turning point was in the Boxing Day Test, after Warne had been omitted from the drawn first Test at Brisbane. With the West Indies comfortably placed at 1-143 when chasing a 359-run target, Warne delivered an impressive flipper that deceived West Indian captain Richie Richardson and bowled him. Warne went on to claim 7-52 and be the hero of Australia's 139-run victory. After Australia came within a whisker of winning the Adelaide Test, which would have clinched the series, Warne was on a losing series on home soil; remarkably, he was never part of another losing series Down Under. Despite his Melbourne heroics, his series figures of 10 wickets at 31.30 were nothing special even if they were a vast improvement from a year earlier.

Australia's 1993 tour of New Zealand, however, was a vastly different story as Warne took 17 scalps at 15.06 in a drawn series, with best figures of 4-8. It finally seemed that he was a long-term investment in the leg-spin department. A couple of years later, New Zealand's Martin Crowe remarked in *Out on a Limb: My own story* that he couldn't believe the transformation in Warne's form since the opening tour match: 'There he had seemed so out of control and inexperienced that I thought he could be just another flash in the pan. But over the next month I watched closely as Border used him cleverly, encouraging him into bowling leg-spin as I'd never seen it before. Not only was his control outstanding but he began to unleash a brilliant variety of destructive deliveries. It was so exciting to see such a talent, even though he sat on the other side.'

The third and most prominent turning point in Warne's career took place at Manchester in the first Test of the 1993 Ashes. He was given his first bowl in an Ashes Test when England was 1-80 in reply to Australia's modest 289. Warne's first delivery pitched well outside leg stump before spinning viciously and clipping the top of a bemused Mike Gatting's off stump. It has often been described as 'the ball of the century'. Certainly the England players were dumbfounded, and the dismissal had a massive psychological effect on them. Warne took 34 wickets at 25.79 and Australia won the series 4-1, while on tour he took 75 first-class scalps at 22.64. The Gatting dismissal in the first Test seemingly overshadowed other pieces of brilliant bowling,

including a delivery that bowled Graham Gooch around his legs.

With fast bowlers having often been the main wicket-takers in international cricket for quite a number of years, Warne proved a revelation in more ways than one. As Gideon Haigh reported on *Cricinfo*: 'Warne was an extraordinary bowler. It can't really be said often enough. He will personify legbreak bowling for as long as the skill exists. If and when an outstanding new purveyor achieves note, the question will be: how does he compare with Warne?'

As Australia trounced New Zealand and drew South Africa on Australian soil in 1993-94, Warne amassed 36 wickets at an average of just 17 in six Tests, yet his match figures of 12-128 at Sydney couldn't prevent the Proteas stealing an improbable five-run victory. As Australia and South Africa had another 1-all drawn series, this time in South Africa, Warne captured 15 wickets at 22.40. He also proved a quality bowler in limited overs cricket, at a time when it was rare for any team to include a leg-spinner in one-day matches. Yet it was during the 1994 South African tour – Allan Border's last hurrah in international cricket – that something didn't

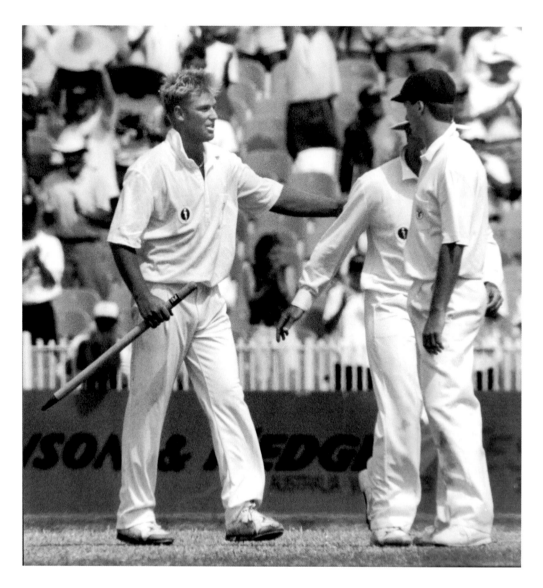

Warne (far left) souvenirs a stump after taking 7-52 to set up an Australian victory against the West Indies in Melbourne in the 1992-93 season.

reflect well on Warne. He was fined for abusing Andrew Hudson after dismissing him, albeit after Warne had been subjected to some abusive behaviour from unruly spectators. Warne was quoted in Allan Miller's 1993-94 cricket annual as saying: 'The continual ride over the past 18 months has got to me and I'm just burning up. I feel angry all the time but I don't want to carry a bad boy reputation for doing one stupid thing.'

Warne needed to get used to enormous publicity, as he became a favourite for media attention. As the years wore on he came under the microscope for things that were by no means unusual in normal everyday life, but became synonymous with Warne. 'Not only is he a smoker, but I've never seen an international cricketer with poorer eating habits. Fruit and vegetables have never been known to pass his lips … Basically he eats the way we all ate as teenagers', Border wrote in *The Dominators.* Extramarital affairs also catapulted Warne into the headlines at various stages, yet he never seemed to show any remorse at his actions or think he should change his ways.

Warne's 18 wickets couldn't prevent Pakistan from winning a three-match series 1-0 in Pakistan in September-October 1994, although Australia would have won the first Test – rather than lose it by one wicket – had a stumping chance not gone begging off Warne's bowling. In the 1994-95 Ashes, Warne took 3-39 and 8-71 at Brisbane, and then 6-64 and 3-16 at his beloved Melbourne Cricket Ground. Warne claimed a hat-trick at Melbourne with Phil DeFreitas lbw, Darren Gough caught behind and Devon Malcolm brilliantly caught by a diving David Boon at short leg. Strangely, Warne took only seven wickets at 51.29 in the remaining

three Tests, with paceman Craig McDermott being Australia's leading bowler. Malcolm slogged Warne for two sixes and two fours in the third Test, and a couple of years later another batting bunny, West Indian Patterson Thompson, clubbed a six off Warne at Adelaide and was reported to have said: 'Hey, I thought this guy was supposed to be a legend.'

Naturally enough, batsmen were just as likely to score runs off Warne than any other bowler, but Warne had something extra that very few – if any – bowlers have possessed. Adept at delivering wrong 'uns, flippers, sliders, top spinners, zooters and regulation leg-breaks as well as other deliveries that defy description, Warne always had batsmen guessing. It wasn't just his unpredictability, but rather something hard to describe as it appeared that he could produce a wicket at virtually any time. 'Warne was no more to be considered simply a bowler than Marilyn Monroe was to be deemed merely as an actress. He was a presence, on the field, in the game, in the media, in the mind. To each delivery, there was a whole preamble, sometimes theatrical, sometimes languorous,

A useful batsman, Warne scored two centuries in first-class cricket but none in Test cricket, although he was unluckily dismissed for 99 on one occasion.

Warne needed to get used to enormous publicity, becoming a favourite for media attention.

always captivating. As he dawdled before his trademark saunter, he would curl the ball from hand to hand, an action both predatory and dainty, feeling his own powers of torque communicated through the ball, keeping the batsman in his crouch that little longer than perhaps was comfortable – time for thought, time for doubt. That pause: it was almost imperceptible, yet time would seem to stand still,' Gideon Haigh reported on *Cricinfo*.

Australia's pacemen were more responsible than Warne for Australia winning back the Frank Worrell Trophy in the Caribbean in 1995, although the leg-spinner played his part with 15 scalps at 27.07. At home in 1995-96, Warne couldn't bowl in the Hobart Test due to a foot injury he had sustained when batting, but his bowling in the Brisbane and Sydney Tests was excellent. He claimed 7-23 and 4-54 at Brisbane, where the hosts won by an innings,

and his two four-wicket hauls in Sydney were in a losing cause but not before Australia had secured a series win. Against Sri Lanka he wasn't quite as effective, but he could hardly be faulted as he had become the first player to take at least 50 Test wickets in a calendar year for three consecutive years: 72 in 1993, 70 in 1994 and 52 in 1995. 'He has lifted the self-esteem of the nation, inspired countless thousands of young cricketers and converted hundreds of thousands of non-cricket fans into watching the game,' Allan Miller wrote of Warne in his 1996 Australian cricket annual.

Following a reduction in Australia's Test schedule in 1996, Warne claimed 15 wickets in just four Tests that year and missed a one-off Test in India due to surgery on a spinning finger. He was one of Australia's best bowlers in the World Cup in the subcontinent but he was hit around in the decider, which Sri Lanka won comfortably. Against the West Indies in season 1996-97, Warne – as in the previous series against the West Indies – played his part without being a standout, capturing 22 wickets at 27. There was one particularly magical delivery, when the left-handed

'Warne was no more to be considered simply a bowler than Marilyn Monroe was to be deemed merely as an actress.'

Shivnarine Chanderpaul was bowled after the ball spun viciously out of the rough.

Warne played his part in series victories in South Africa and England in 1997, and was Australia's leading wicket-taker in a home series win against New Zealand later in the year. Warne's six wickets against South Africa in the Boxing Day Test took his tally for the year to 68, and then his 11 scalps in the Sydney Test in the opening week of 1998 enabled him to reach the milestone of 300 Test wickets. It had taken Warne almost exactly six years to reach the 300 figure, and at the age of 28 he was already quickly approaching Dennis Lillee's Australian record of 355 Test wickets.

However, the rest of 1998 was not so favourable for Warne. In India, where Australia was thrashed in two Tests before winning the dead rubber, Warne took just 10 wickets at 54. He then underwent shoulder surgery in May, and missed Australia's series win in

Pakistan and most of Australia's 1998-99 Ashes series triumph at home. Warne's replacement, Stuart MacGill, proved to be just as good as Warne even if his style was different. Warne's comeback was in the New Year Test of 1999 and, although Warne claimed a wicket in his first over in each innings, MacGill was the star. Warne's match figures of 2-110 from 39 overs paled compared with MacGill's 12-107 from 40.2 overs. The 1998-99 season proved a blight on the careers of both Warne and Mark Waugh, as it was discovered they had accepted money from an Indian bookmaker in 1994. Both players were fined, and that was virtually the end of the matter.

Australia's tour of the West Indies in 1999 was another less than happy time for Warne, who claimed just two wickets at 134 in the first three Tests. Captain Steve Waugh and coach Geoff Marsh, who played in Warne's first two Tests, chose to omit Warne from the fourth and final Test. Although the combination of Glenn McGrath, Adam Dale, Colin Miller and MacGill shared 17 wickets in an Australian victory that salvaged a drawn series, Warne seemingly held a grudge against Steve Waugh thereafter.

Still in the Caribbean in 1999, Warne nonetheless bowled well in

Warne at training.

the limited overs fixtures following the Test series, then he shone in Australia's winning World Cup campaign with 20 wickets at 18.05, including 4-29 in the semi-final and 4-33 in the decider. The selectors dropped the unlucky MacGill later in the year, and Warne captured eight wickets at 14.38 in a series loss in Sri Lanka before taking six scalps in a one-off Test in Zimbabwe. With Australia winning all six Tests on home soil in 1999-2000 – three against Pakistan and three against India – Warne took a modest 20 wickets at 35.25. The leg-spinner

nevertheless needed only five more scalps to overtake Lillee's Test wickets tally. Warne achieved the feat in New Zealand, notching 15 wickets in a 3-0 clean-sweep in early 2000.

A finger injury sustained when taking a catch forced Warne to miss Australia's 5-0 drubbing of the West Indies in 2000-01. Returning for the 2001 Indian tour Warne again struggled, with figures similar to those he achieved in the same country in 1998. England, however, was again a happy hunting ground, with Warne's 31 wickets at 18.71 taking him past 400 Test wickets.

Warne picked up 58 Test wickets in 2001 and 67 in 2002. He claimed just six wickets in three Tests when Australia and New Zealand drew 0-all Down Under in late 2001, then he captured 17 victims in a 3-0 whitewash of South Africa. Warne did even better in South Africa in early 2002, notching 20 wickets, and later in the year he was more damaging in Pakistan. In this tour he nabbed 27 wickets in the three Tests, before taking 14 in three Tests in the 2002-03 Ashes but then missing two Tests with injury. In early 2003, his career was in jeopardy as he earned a 12-month suspension for using a banned diuretic. His tally of Test wickets stood at 491.

Warne was still able to reproduce his magic when he notched 70 Test wickets in 2004 and a phenomenal 96 the following year. Warne was temporarily Test cricket's leading wicket-taker, before Sri Lanka's Muttiah Muralitharan finished with 800 scalps to Warne's 708. Interestingly, before Warne even played first-class cricket, former Australian fast bowler Rodney Hogg was sacked from his position with *The Truth* newspaper for remarking that Warne would capture 500 Test wickets. Who would have thought

Hogg's prediction would seem conservative?

In Warne's return to Tests, he claimed four consecutive five-wicket hauls and finished the series with 26 scalps at 20.04 in a 3-0 drubbing of Sri Lanka on Sri Lankan turf, while Muralitharan captured 28 wickets at 23.18. Later in the year, Warne had easily his most successful tour of India when he claimed 14 wickets at 30.07 as Australia won a Test series in India for the first time since 1969-70. In early 2005, Warne played his last one-day international but still had another two years of Test cricket in him.

After taking 25 scalps in five Tests at home in 2004-05 and a further 17 scalps in three Tests in New Zealand, Warne captured 40 wickets at 19.93 in the 2005 Ashes. It wasn't enough to prevent England winning the Ashes for the first time since 1986-87 but, as Warne was nearing his 36th birthday and his marriage was all but over, his bowling was as potent as ever.

Warne deserved a lot of credit for keeping Australia in the hunt for the Ashes as England was the better side for the greater part of the series, although he dropped a catch in the final Test, which was drawn.

The New Zealanders enjoy the dismissal of Warne for 99 in the Perth Test in late 2001. Mark Richardson (second from right) held an outfield catch from a kamikaze stroke off the bowling of Daniel Vettori (second from left), before a replay showed that the delivery should have been called a no-ball.

That missed chance, along with a dropped slips catch in late 1999 that prevented Damien Fleming taking what would have been a second Test hat-trick, were two notable errors Warne made in the field. (Interestingly, Warne's maiden first-class wicket involved Tom Moody being caught by Fleming. Less than 10 years later, the three players were World Cup winning team-mates.) In any case, Warne was predominantly a reliable slips fielder. Also in the 2005 Ashes, he came within 10 runs of scoring a maiden Test century. In late 2001, he holed out to deep mid wicket on 99 from a delivery that replays revealed should have been called a no-ball. Unluckily, Warne ultimately finished with the most runs by a Test batsman who had never scored a century.

Warne was still able to reproduce his magic when he notched 70 Test wickets in 2004 and a phenomenal 96 the following year.

Following the 2005 Ashes, Warne played key roles in series wins against the West Indies, South Africa and Bangladesh, before the 2006-07 Ashes signalled the end of his international career. Warne captured 23 wickets at 30.35 in Australia's 5-0 whitewash, with a number of highlights. He claimed the final wicket of the third Test at Perth to seal the series and reach 699 Test wickets. He chalked up 700 when he bowled England opener Andrew Strauss at Melbourne, capturing 5-39 and 2-46 in his penultimate Test. Two wickets in his final Test enabled Warne to finish with 1001 international wickets, while his 195 wickets against England were the highest by a bowler against one country in Test cricket. According to Haigh, Warne's performances in his last few years 'bordered on burlesque.

The Ashes of 2005 and 2006-07 were series divided: there was the cricket featuring Warne, then the rest. There was brilliance, there was bluff; he was the beamish boy one moment, the blowhard the next. He was seldom outbowled, hardly outfoxed, never out-talked ...'

While Warne's team-mates have rarely bagged him too much, at least publicly, Warne never hesitated to voice his disapproval of certain individuals. Because of his axing in the Caribbean in 1999, Warne considered Steve Waugh the most selfish cricketer he ever played alongside. Warne was also known to joust with John Buchanan during Buchanan's stint as Australian coach. During boot camp in the lead-up to Warne's final Test series, Warne got away with breaking the rules when he brought his cigarettes with him. As Matthew Hayden reported in *Standing My Ground*: 'I laughed at the incident – you just had to – because that defiant side of Warnie always cracked me up. Great talent often comes with a bit of rebelliousness ... After Buck retired as national coach in 2007, he said that Warnie's brutal honesty was one of the qualities he most admired about him. As shamelessly rebellious

Warne appeals for a wicket during a Test match.

as Warnie could be, it actually made him easier to deal with than some other athletes – you knew exactly where you stood.'

The last words about Warne go to Christian Ryan, who reported in Warne's *Cricinfo* profile: 'When Warne likened his life to a soap opera, he was selling himself short. His story was part fairytale, part pantomime, part hospital drama, part adult's-only romp, part glittering awards ceremony … Maybe, as with Posh Spice or Kylie Minogue, Warne is more famous than he is loved … One thing's for sure, though. Cricket was poorer for his going.'

Career statistics

	Tests	One-day internationals	First-class matches
Matches	145	194	301
Innings	199	107	404
Not outs	17	29	48
Runs scored	3,154	1,018	6,919
Batting average	17.33	13.05	19.44
100s / 50s	0 / 12	0 / 1	2 / 26
Top score	99	55	107*
Balls bowled	40,705	10, 642	74,830
Runs	17,995	7,541	34,449
Wickets	708	293	1,319
Bowling average	25.42	25.74	26.12
5 wickets in an innings	37	1	69
10 wickets in a match	10	n/a	12
Best bowling	8/71 (12/128)	5 / 33	8 / 71
Catches	125	80	264

A classic snapshot of Dennis Lillee's marvellous bowling action.

DENNIS LILLEE

Birth date	18 July 1949
Place of birth	Subiaco, Perth, Western Australia
Nickname/s	FOT (flippin' old tart)
Playing role	Right arm fast bowler

A big-hearted fast bowler with plenty of mongrel while also being an entertaining cricketer, Dennis Lillee was the first Australian to reach the milestone of 300 Test wickets and the third overall bowler to achieve the milestone – after Englishman Fred Trueman and West Indian Lance Gibbs.

Despite the notable increase in the amount of Test cricket played in most years since Lillee's playing days, as of late 2018 Shane Warne and Glenn McGrath have been the only Australians to exceed his wicket-taking tally. Wicketkeeper Rod Marsh held 95 of his 355 Test dismissals (with the gloves) off Lillee's bowling.

Lillee had the rare ability to adjust to whatever type of pitch or conditions he encountered, and he made the most of the situation. A match-winner who generated plenty of passion among onlookers, Lillee brought the crowds to life: there were often chants of 'Lill-ee, Lill-ee, Lill-ee' or 'Kill, kill, kill' during

matches. His larrikin-like nature also endeared him to many Australian fans. He was able to unsettle and even terrorise players from virtually any team as he was a real 'in your face' type. Against players of the highest class in the form of Garry Sobers, Viv Richards, Ian Botham and Sunil Gavaskar, Lillee sometimes dismissed them although they also scored their fair share of runs off him. It often made for an intriguing contest.

In Allan Border's first autobiography, Border commented: 'Fot's outstanding quality was his fierce competitiveness. Fast bowlers traditionally take the game ultra-seriously, but I have never

A fiery fast bowler and entertainer, Lillee enthralled Australian crowds in the 1970s and early 1980s.

Lillee had the rare ability to adjust to whatever type of pitch or conditions he encountered . . .

seen a more intensely competitive spirit than that possessed by D.K. Lillee.' Pakistani great Imran Khan considered that: 'Lillee's greatest asset was that he would rise to the occasion, especially in front of those huge crowds at the Melbourne Cricket Ground, getting life out of the dreadful pitches they had there at the time,' as documented in his book *All Round View*. Imran deemed that 'the sign of an outstanding player is his ability to perform well consistently under pressure. He must also be a complete team man'. Imran immediately went on to say that 'the bowler who really stands out is Dennis Lillee'.

Lillee's hostility, combative nature, competitive streak and fierce determination were perhaps never better exemplified than in a one-day match for his home state in December 1976. Hosts Western Australia were skittled for just 77

against Queensland, before Lillee inspired a miracle. He peppered Viv Richards with some short-pitched deliveries and then, incredibly, bowled the West Indian import with a half-volley to have Queensland a wicket down without a run on the board. Bowling like a man possessed, Lillee also dismissed his Australian captain and team-mate Greg Chappell, and finished with 4-21 to play the chief role in Western Australia's shock 15-run victory.

In a *WA Today* article in 2016 (www.watoday.com.au/wa-news/dennis-lillees-search-for-his-greatest-inspiration-his-primary-school-teacher-20161110-gsmnri.html), Lillee rated one of his primary school teachers – Ken Waters – as his biggest influence. Lillee said: 'Ken was a very fit guy who taught us football, athletics and cricket.

'More than that, the fierce determination in him rubbed off on us and he wasn't just about playing the game, it was about winning.

'There was something I learnt about life ... life's not just about playing the game, it is about winning.'

By his own admission, Lillee had white line fever when competing,

Lawrence Rowe plays a hook shot off Lillee's bowling during a World Series Cricket match in the late 1970s.

but was more carefree when on the other side of the line. The outswinger was Lillee's stock delivery in his early years, but his variety improved as he cut the ball both ways and could also bowl bouncers and yorkers. Lillee debuted for Western Australia in 1969-70 and was the state's leading wicket-taker, bowling with impressive pace despite being a raw 20-year-old. The following season he was brought into the Australian side for the last two Tests of the Ashes, with England leading the series 1-0. On debut at Adelaide, Lillee's first victim was England opener John Edrich, who scored 130. His next victim was Alan Knott, who became the batsman to succumb most often to Lillee in Tests: 12 times. Lillee claimed 5-84 from 28.3 overs as England racked up 470 in a match that was heading for a draw, before the tourists won the Sydney Test to claim the Ashes for the first time in 12 years.

Lillee finished the two Tests with eight wickets at 24.88, and the following season he claimed 8-29 in a fixture against the Rest of the World XI at Perth. As Garry Sobers documented in *Garry Sobers: My autobiography*: 'The first ball Lillee bowled, Gavaskar went forward, the ball took off and went past his head at an incredible rate of knots. All the fellows in the dressing room immediately started to volunteer for the 9, 10 and 11 positions in the batting order ... Dennis had 0-11 overnight and finished up with 8 for 29. I had never seen anything like it. The laws of gravity tell you that if a moving object hits anything it must slow down. You often hear a commentator saying the ball quickened off the wicket but that is only a figure of speech. But this wicket was quick and bouncy and it really looked as though the ball was taking off after it had pitched.'

Lillee was the leading wicket-taker in the 1972 Ashes series in England, with 31 scalps at 17.68, although England retained the Ashes. Lillee nonetheless bagged two five-wicket hauls in the final Test to ensure the tourists at least drew the series. Several months later, Lillee took 12 wickets at 29.42 as Australia won 3-0 against Pakistan, although he suffered a back complaint. Imran Khan nonetheless noted that Lillee insisted on bowling, albeit off a shorter run, and that in the Sydney Test he helped dismiss Pakistan when the tourists were in the position to win. As Imran wrote in *All Round View:* 'Most other bowlers in this situation would have given up, and his refusal to do so makes Lillee number one in my book.'

However, Lillee's back injury turned into a major worry. He played just one Test in Australia's 1972-73 tour of the Caribbean, not taking a single wicket while conceding 132 runs in 32 overs. Australia nonetheless went on to win the five-match series 2-0, although stress fractures threatened to end Lillee's career. Following extensive rehabilitation, Lillee remodelled his action and returned to the Test arena for the 1974-75 Ashes.

Fellow fast bowler Jeff Thomson, with a wild slinging action that generated ferocious pace, formed a deadly combination with Lillee as Australia romped to a 4-1 series triumph. Thomson also had some injury problems during his career, but from 1974 to 1977 the combination of Lillee and Thomson

However, Lillee's back injury turned into a major worry.

achieved 149 wickets in 15 Tests at an average slightly above 25. Thomson was the main destroyer in the 1974-75 Ashes, claiming 33 wickets at 17.94 in the first five Tests before missing the sixth with injury.

Lillee consistently claimed two wickets per innings until he bagged two four-wicket hauls in the fifth Test, and his series figures were 25 wickets at 23.84. He was injured during the final Test, which England won by an innings as the tourists profited from the absence of Australia's two strike bowlers. When Australia won the Ashes 1-0 in a four-match series in England a little later in 1975, Thomson was not quite as prominent, claiming 16 scalps at 28.56. As he had done four years earlier, Lillee topped the series' wicket-taking aggregates, this time with 21 victims at 21.90 each.

A statue of Lillee's bowling action was installed at the Melbourne Cricket Ground.

Thomson and Lillee were again Australia's best bowlers on home soil when Australia contested the West Indies in 1975-76, with 29 and 27 wickets respectively in the home team's 5-1 victory. Disaster struck against Pakistan the following season, when Thomson badly injured his shoulder in a fielding mishap. Australia had to settle for a 1-all result in the three-Test series, with Lillee capturing 21 wickets: the next best Australian bowler was Kerry O'Keeffe, with 11 scalps. Lillee claimed 11 wickets in a Test at Auckland to help the Australians to a 1-0 series win against their Trans-Tasman rivals, before his career highlight at the Centenary Test at Melbourne in March 1977. His 6-26 helped rout England for 95 after Australia tallied 138, then he captured 5-139 as Australia won by 45 runs. It was an identical result to that of the inaugural Test.

Lillee's battle with Derek Randall was particularly eye-catching. Randall was caught behind off Lillee for 4 in England's first innings before ducking and weaving and also scoring runs against some hostile fast bowling in the second innings, as Randall's 174 threatened to set up an improbable England victory. Lillee then took a rest, and Australia badly missed him as England won the 1977 Ashes 3-0 at home.

The Centenary Test was Lillee's last Test for nearly three years due to his joining World Series Cricket, in which he claimed 79 wickets in unofficial Tests. Upon his return to the Test arena, 'Lillee earned his wickets with control and swing rather than sheer speed, although he was never short of being genuinely fast', wrote Peter Arnold in *The Illustrated Encyclopedia of World Cricket.*

In their home Tests in 1979-80, the Australians lost 2-0 to the West Indies before clean-sweeping England 3-0. Lillee was the home side's leading wicket-taker in both series, although his 12 wickets at 30.42 in three Tests against the West Indies were overshadowed by the touring team's pacemen. Colin Croft, Joel Garner, Michael Holding and Andy Roberts formed a destructive quartet. During the subsequent series Lillee claimed 23 wickets at 16.87, although the Ashes were not at stake.

Lillee's most unproductive series was in Pakistan in early 1980, with the hosts winning the three-match

. . . Lillee feigned an injury at practice in front of the Pakistanis . . .

series 1-0. As Allan Border wrote in his 1986 autobiography: 'It must be stressed that he was obliged to toil on wickets not only unsuited to him but deliberately prepared that way.' After Pakistan won the first Test at Karachi on what Border described as a 'raging turner of a wicket', the pitches at Faisalabad and Lahore were very flat and conducive to scoring runs. At Lahore, the tourists found that two pitches had been prepared: a very grassy strip and a very bare strip. Wanting to play on the grassy surface, the Australians devised a devious ploy that proved to be all in vain: Lillee feigned an injury at practice in front of the Pakistanis, and four team-mates 'carted him off the ground like a fallen warrior', as Border described.

Border said the plan had been to circulate the lie that the Australians would fly in Ashley Mallett from Australia to replace Lillee. 'Hopefully, the Pakis would swallow this load of nonsense and decide that since the major threat to their batsmen was sidelined, the Test would be played on the well-grassed wicket. Then, on the morning of the match, we would declare Dennis fit. Miraculous recovery and all that … Unfortunately, the Pakistanis did not fall for our little game and the Test was played on that bare flat wicket,' Border wrote. After bowling 39 overs in the Karachi Test and 21 overs in the Faisalabad Test without taking any wickets, Lillee claimed 3-114 from 42 overs in the Lahore Test.

In a series win at home against New Zealand in 1980-81, Lillee nabbed 16 wickets at 15.31 before getting 21 scalps at 21.52 in a drawn series with India. While Ian Botham earned plenty of accolades for England's 3-1 Ashes win in 1981, when Australia failed to grasp winning opportunities, Lillee nonetheless claimed 39 scalps at 22.31 in the six Tests. However, Lillee's Western Australian team-mate Terry Alderman was the leading bowler, with 42 wickets. Lillee's 15 wickets were second to Bruce Yardley's 18, with Australia beating Pakistan 2-1 Down Under in 1981-82, while Imran claimed 16 wickets for Pakistan. In the subsequent drawn series with the West Indies, Lillee had 16 scalps to Yardley's 20, while Holding had 24 for the tourists.

*Lillee gives Australian pace bowler Glenn McGrath some advice during
a training session.*

As Australia was on its way to winning the first Test in Melbourne by 58 runs, Lillee claimed his best innings figures in Test cricket (7-83) before taking 3-44 in the West Indies' second innings. After a brilliant Kim Hughes century helped the Australians to a still sub-standard 198, Lillee took three quick wickets to have the tourists 4-10 at stumps. With the last ball of the day he bowled Richards off an inside edge, and the next day he became Test cricket's leading wicket-taker when Larry Gomes edged a slips catch to Greg Chappell.

Lillee snared 15 wickets at 22.13 as hosts Pakistan whitewashed Australia 3-0 in late 1982, before a knee injury curtailed his 1982-83 summer. The drawn first Test at Perth was Lillee's only Test that season; he took 3-96 and 1-89, while Alderman injured his shoulder as he tackled a pitch invader and then couldn't play for the rest of the series. The hosts nonetheless went on to win the series 2-1, with Geoff

Lillee prepares to rocket down another delivery.

Lawson, Thomson and Yardley the main wicket-takers.

Lillee took three wickets in a one-off Test against Sri Lanka in 1983, before the 1983-84 season was his last in Test cricket as he farewelled the international scene alongside Greg Chappell and Rod Marsh. Lillee took only one wicket in the first two Tests, then took 6-171 and showed impressive stamina by sending down 50.2 overs while Pakistan amassed 624 in the drawn Adelaide Test. Following five wickets in Melbourne, Lillee claimed 4-65 and 4-88 in his farewell, which Australia won by 10 wickets to seal a 2-0 series victory. Lillee had the honour of taking a wicket with his final delivery, Sarfraz Nawaz being caught by Wayne Phillips. Chappell scored 182 and Marsh 15 not out, and the trio were also among the catches as Lillee held two, Chappell three and Marsh six.

Lillee's Test career could be broken into three parts: the period before he succumbed to his back injury, the period from the 1974-75 Ashes until World Series Cricket, and then the time frame from 1979-80 to his final Test. His figures showed a great deal of consistency. From his Test debut until his exit

from the Caribbean tour in early 1973, Lillee took 51 wickets at 24.16 from 11 Tests. From late 1974 until March 1977 he snared 120 scalps at 23.20 from 21 Tests, before nabbing 184 victims at 24.32 in his 38 Tests from December 1979. In the calendar year of 1981, he achieved 85 Test scalps. He claimed 231 wickets from 44 Tests on home soil and 124 wickets from 26 Tests away from home, while against England he had 167 scalps from 29 Tests.

A lower order batsman, Lillee sometimes made some useful runs. His best Test score of 73 not out was at number 10 during an Ashes Test at Lord's in 1975, as Lillee helped Australia go from 8-133 to 268 all out via partnerships of 66 and 69. His record in one-day internationals was also exceptionally good, with 103 wickets at 20.83 from 63 appearances.

It was hardly surprising that someone with Lillee's temperament and demeanour would find himself at the centre of controversy from time to time. In the Perth Test of 1979-80, Lillee experimented with an aluminium bat and was forced to replace it after England captain Mike Brearley claimed it damaged the ball. Lillee was resistant at first,

It was hardly surprising that someone with Lillee's temperament and demeanour would find himself at the centre of controversy from time to time.

before throwing the bat away in fury and resuming his innings with the traditional willow.

During the 1981 Ashes, Lillee and Marsh placed a wager in the third Test at Headingley, as odds of an England win were rated 500-1 when the hosts were seven wickets down in their second innings and still 92 runs in arrears. England ended up recording a staggering 18-run victory, and although their wager became widely publicised Lillee and Marsh received no official punishment. In the years since, similar actions have been scrutinised a great deal, with some players earning lengthy suspensions and even life bans.

The third major controversy involving Lillee was against Pakistan at Perth in 1981-82 as he had a minor collision with Javed Miandad, who was running between the wickets. Miandad was renowned during a long and largely successful

international career for getting under the skin of team-mates as well as opponents, and Lillee was unhappy with his antics. Following the collision, Lillee walked up to Miandad and deliberately kicked him, prompting the Pakistani to raise his bat and threaten to retaliate. Umpire Tony Crafter bravely sandwiched himself between the combatants. Lillee's actions were roundly criticised, and the punishment was a suspension from two one-day internationals.

Despite the demands of international cricket, Lillee took almost as many first-class wickets for his state as he claimed Test wickets for his country. Lillee snared 351 first-class wickets from 76 appearances for Western Australia from 1969-70 until 1984, and then claimed 16 wickets at 37.50 from six appearances for Tasmania in 1987-88. Lillee was fined for an off-field indiscretion that also involved Botham, who played for Queensland that season.

In retirement, Lillee was involved in helping to develop up-and-coming fast bowlers, even opening a fast bowling school in India. At the age of 41, he played for the Western Australian Cricket Association's President's XI against an England XI in a tour match at

Lilac Hill Park in Perth. His figures of 9-0-47-0 were nothing to write home about, although he became a regular fixture in the annual tour match at Lilac Hill Park as the host team became the ACB Chairman's XI. Lillee had mixed fortunes in this series of limited overs matches, finishing on a high at the age of 50. He opened the bowling with his son Adam against Pakistan, with the father taking 3-8 from eight overs while the son took 3-29 from six overs. Adam also took a spectacular catch off his famous father's bowling.

Career statistics

	Tests	One-day internationals	First-class matches
Matches	70	63	198
Innings	90	34	241
Not outs	24	8	70
Runs scored	905	240	2,377
Batting average	13.71	9.23	13.90
100s / 50s	0 / 1	0 / 0	0 / 2
Top score	73*	42*	73*
Balls bowled	18,467	3,593	44,806
Runs	8,493	2,145	20,695
Wickets	355	103	882
Bowling average	23.92	20.83	23.46
5 wickets in an innings	23	1	50
10 wickets in a match	7	n/a	13
Best bowling	7/83 (11/123)	5 / 34	8 / 29
Catches	23	10	67

Glenn McGrath in action during the 2006-07 Ashes, his final Test series.

11

GLENN McGRATH

Birth date	9 February 1970
Place of birth	Dubbo, New South Wales
Nickname/s	Pigeon, Millard
Playing role	Right arm fast-medium bowler

'He is one of the all-time greats, and if there was a fast bowler I had to pick in my team to take the field any day of the week, it would be McGrath. If I was given a choice from every other country or every other era, it would be Glenn McGrath, hands down.'

Ricky Ponting made this assertion in Glenn McGrath's biography *Line and Strength*, having played international cricket with McGrath for the best part of a decade and captained Australia in the last few years of McGrath's career. Ponting's assertion may seem a big statement, given the reputations of other candidates such as Dennis Lillee and numerous West Indian pacemen from the 1970s through to the 1990s. Nonetheless, McGrath became only the second pace bowler to top 500 Test wickets while, astonishingly, he was able to remember the batsman and mode of dismissal for each of them. As Lillee remarked in *Line and Strength*:

'McGrath had a machine-like action that was economical *and* easy on the body.'

McGrath's main strengths were that he consistently bowled accurately and with a great line and length, and gained movement off the wicket. He was able to hit the stumps and rap batsmen on the pads, as well as find the edge of the bat for catches to the wicketkeeper and slips cordon. These assets proved more decisive than speed, which was an interesting if obscure aspect of McGrath's career. He was regarded as a fast bowler, and although he sometimes bowled at around 140 kilometres per hour, he often bowled between 130 and

McGrath bowls during a Test on home soil.

McGrath's main strengths were that he consistently bowled accurately and with a great line and length . . .

135 kilometres per hour. When speed guns were introduced in the late 1990s, it was revealed that McGrath bowled at the same pace as Australian team-mate Greg Blewett, who was regarded as a part-time medium-pacer.

Although McGrath rarely bowled in tandem with Shane Warne, Australia's bowling stocks were always formidable with the two of them in the team. They played 104 Tests together, with Australia winning 71 and losing just 18; Warne nabbed 513 wickets to McGrath's 488. Warne was the second Australian to notch 300 Test scalps and the first Australian to notch 400, 500, 600 and 700, while McGrath was the next Australian after Warne to reach the 300, 400 and 500 milestones. McGrath nabbed his 100th Test scalp just over three years after his debut, and then it took only another two years for him to double that tally. It took less than two years for McGrath to go from 200 to 300, and within another two years he notched 400; nearly three years passed between the 400 and 500 milestones.

Interestingly, McGrath didn't take up cricket seriously until he was a teenager. Playing for Dubbo against Parkes at Parkes in the Tooheys Country Cup Challenge in late 1988, McGrath claimed 3-44 in a match that featured Doug Walters, Mark Waugh, Mark Taylor and Greg Matthews as guests. Walters promptly advised Steve Rixon from the New

South Wales Cricket Association that a particular bowler from Dubbo was worthy of attention. McGrath moved from the country and played club cricket for Sutherland, and at one stage lived in a caravan. He attended the Australian Cricket Academy, and made his first-class debut shortly before his 23rd birthday in the early part of 1993. Adam Gilchrist made his first-class debut in the same match, scoring 16 for New South Wales, while Ponting notched his maiden first-class century for Tasmania. McGrath claimed a wicket in his third over before he conceded a run, and went on to record great figures of 29.1-9-79-5. In Tasmania's second innings he had 0-29, but was unable to complete his 14th over due to a thigh injury.

After helping New South Wales win the first-class and limited overs domestic competitions in the 1992-93 season, McGrath found himself in Australia's Test and one-day teams the following summer. He quickly became a success in the shorter form of the game, as he was a consistent wicket-taker while rarely being expensive. He continued this throughout his career but his first 12 months in Test cricket were patchy at best. McGrath claimed

> McGrath didn't take up cricket seriously until he was a teenager.

2-92 and 1-50 on debut as Australia contested New Zealand at Perth, but had to carry the drinks in half of the six Tests in Australia during the 1993-94 season. He took 0-45 and 3-66 in his second appearance, and against South Africa claimed 1-32 and 1-30. McGrath played in two of the three Tests in Australia's subsequent tour of South Africa, taking four wickets while usually bowling at first change after sharing the new ball with Craig McDermott on home soil.

McGrath played in just two of five Ashes Tests in 1994-95, the first and last Tests of the series. He conceded 101 runs in 29 wicketless overs at Brisbane before having match figures of 6-128 from 38 overs at Perth, where Australia secured a 3-1 series victory. Following his failure at Brisbane, McGrath deemed that his problem was not hitting the crease hard enough, as well as trying to swing the ball rather than bowl normally. At Perth he twice accounted for England captain and opening batsman Mike Atherton.

McGrath dismissed Atherton a further 17 times in Test cricket, with 10 of the 19 dismissals being caught behind. There was only one lbw and none were bowled.

Australia's 1995 tour of the West Indies proved a decisive turning point in McGrath's career as the tourists missed injured duo McDermott and Damien Fleming. McGrath was Australia's leading wicket-taker in the four-Test series with 17 scalps at 21.71. He was the second change bowler in the first two Tests, and his figures of 3-46 and 5-68 were vital as the tourists won the opening battle. Interestingly, the only Test in which McGrath took the new ball was the third, in which he claimed 6-47 and 0-22 in Australia's nine-wicket loss before taking just two wickets in the series-deciding victory. McGrath dismissed West Indian record-breaking left-handed batsman Brian Lara twice in the series, and would go on to dismiss him another 13 times in Tests.

The 1995-96 season was destined to be McDermott's last but it made little difference to McGrath, who had become Australia's main strike bowler. At this stage he perhaps bowled the quickest that he ever had. In Australia's 15 Tests from October

The Australians flock to congratulate McGrath, who claimed a hat-trick against the West Indies at Perth in late 2000. West Indian skipper Jimmy Adams ruefully exits after being the third victim in the hat-trick, as McGrath went from 298 to 301 Test wickets with three successive deliveries.

1996 to August 1997, McGrath nabbed 77 scalps at a cost of just 19.86 each. In six Tests on home turf in 1995-96, he took 36 wickets at 21.67 as Australia toppled Pakistan and Sri Lanka. In 1996-97, McGrath outshone West Indian pacemen Curtly Ambrose, Courtney Walsh and Ian Bishop, with the Australian picking up 26 wickets at 17.42 while none of the West Indians topped 20 wickets in the five-Test series.

After helping Australia retain the Frank Worrell Trophy in 1996-97, during which time he took his 100th Test scalp, McGrath went on to take 13 wickets in three Tests on South African soil, the tourists winning 2-1. He was also far and away the standout bowler in the 1997 Ashes. McGrath bagged 36 scalps in the six Tests, with Warne and England's Andy Caddick being the next best with 24 wickets apiece.

Jimmy Adams falls victim to McGrath during the 1995 Frank Worrell Trophy series in the Caribbean.

At this stage he perhaps bowled the quickest that he ever had.

McGrath had disappointing match figures of 2-149 from 39 overs in his first Test on England soil as Australia was thrashed. The second Test at Lord's was a vastly different matter, as McGrath took a sensational 8-38 from 20.3 overs to rout England for 77; rain interruptions meant England was dismissed at lunch on day three after batting first. McGrath's figures were the best by an Australian in a Test since Arthur Mailey took 9-121 in an Ashes battle in February 1921. The weather ruined Australia's victory prospects at Lord's before McGrath claimed seven victims in each of the third, fifth and sixth Tests. He snared 7-76 in England's first innings in the dead rubber Test at the Oval, only for the hosts to record a shock 19-run win to salvage a 3-2 series loss.

Groin, stomach and side injuries curtailed McGrath in 1997-98, in

England's Mike Atherton departs after falling to McGrath, one of 19 times McGrath dismissed Atherton in Test cricket.

which he claimed 11 wickets at 24 while playing in only three of Australia's nine Tests. He was sorely missed as Australia crashed to a series loss in India following success against New Zealand and South Africa. Later in the year, McGrath claimed a dozen wickets in three Tests as Australia won a Test series in Pakistan for the first time in nearly 40 years.

The absence of an injured Warne for most of the Tests involving Australia in 1998-99 did not increase the reliability on McGrath, considering Stuart MacGill proved to be just as good as Warne. MacGill took 27 wickets to McGrath's 24 in the Ashes series Down Under, before McGrath took 30 wickets to MacGill's 12 in a drawn series in the Caribbean. McGrath took 18 wickets to Warne's 20 in Australia's 1999 World Cup triumph, as they were among several survivors from Australia's loss to Sri Lanka in the 1996 World Cup decider. McGrath claimed 2-13 from nine overs in the 1999 decider as Australia thrashed Pakistan by eight wickets, and he had no price to pay for dropping a lollipop catch when Pakistan was two wickets down and looking to consolidate.

After Australia lost a series to Sri Lanka for the first time, McGrath was prominent as usual when Australia trounced Zimbabwe in a one-off Test and then accounted for Pakistan, India and New Zealand 3-0. In those 10 Test victories, McGrath tallied 50 wickets at 20 each, with the pick of them being the first Test of 2000 when he took 5-48 and 5-55 against India at Sydney. As Australia slaughtered the West Indies 5-0 in 2000-01, McGrath somewhat underachieved in the last three Tests after being prominent in the first two, both of which the hosts won by an innings. He had match figures of 10-27 from 33 overs at Brisbane, and entered the next Test at Perth on 298 Test wickets. Remarkably, he snared a hat-trick in the first session on day one to reach 301 wickets, accounting for Sherwin Campbell, Brian Lara and West Indies captain Jimmy Adams. The right-handed opener edged a regulation catch to Ponting at first slip before the left-handed Lara edged to fourth slip, where MacGill held a juggling catch. Adams, another left-hander, fended at a brute of a delivery and could only lob a simple catch to Justin Langer at short leg. In the fourth Test at

McGrath and children James and Holly say farewell at the completion of McGrath's final Test, at the Sydney Cricket Ground in January 2007.

McGrath is chaired off the field in triumph as Australia completes a 5-0 Ashes series victory in his final Test series.

Melbourne, McGrath went wicketless for the first time in a Test since the opening Ashes clash six years earlier, but on the latter occasion his figures were respectable as he conceded only 25 runs from as many overs.

McGrath's 17 wickets at 15.35 weren't enough to prevent India coming from behind to win 2-1 on home soil in 2001 before his 32 wickets – coupled with Warne's 31 – helped Australia canter to another Ashes series win. In a 0-all drawn series with New Zealand in late 2001,

McGrath had a rare lean patch as his strike rate of 140.4 was just as uncharacteristic as his five wickets at 65.40. Against South Africa he was back in business, with 14 wickets at 25 on home soil and 12 wickets at 18.92 in the African nation. Australia was just too strong. In an away series win against Pakistan in late 2002, McGrath's 14 scalps cost just 10.86 each, before his form in the Ashes produced 19 wickets at 20. He missed the final Test, which England won after Australia sought a series

. . . McGrath somewhat underachieved in the last three Tests after being prominent in the first two . . .

whitewash. In Australia's undefeated World Cup campaign in South Africa in 2003, McGrath's highlight was 7-15 against minnows Namibia.

Injury restricted McGrath to two Tests in Australia's ensuing Test series in the Caribbean, where he claimed just three scalps at 52.67 each. He was involved in an ugly spat with Ramnaresh Sarwan at St John's in Antigua, when the hosts prevented a 4-0 clean-sweep with the highest successful run chase in Test history. After McGrath took five wickets in a 2-0 clean-sweep of Bangladesh in mid-2003, his international career went into limbo as he underwent two operations on his left ankle and missed a year of international cricket. With Warne also missing for some of that time due to a drug-related suspension, Australia comfortably beat Zimbabwe and drew with India on Australian soil before accounting for Sri Lanka in Sri Lanka. Australia then hosted Sri Lanka for two Tests in the winter of 2004, with McGrath reporting in *The Ashes: Match of My Life* that the series 'was being billed as my last chance to prove I still had a Test career. I was 34 and

few fast bowlers keep going at that age. I was told a leading Australian quick had not started a Test after his 35th birthday for more than four decades'.

Ten wickets at 17.10 in Australia's 2-0 triumph over Sri Lanka showed that McGrath still had plenty of good cricket left in him. 'That year out of the game had been a godsend. Yes, it came with plenty of frustrations, but I never contemplated retiring, it didn't even fleetingly pass through my mind. It was a good break for me, it freshened me up and made me hungry for the game,' he reflected in *The Ashes: Match of My Life*. Later in 2004, McGrath picked up 14 victims at 25.43 as Australia won a series in India for the first time in 35 years, although he felt that he wasn't quite back to his best.

Having taken nine wickets in a 2-0 drubbing of New Zealand, McGrath subsequently claimed 8-24 in a thrashing of Pakistan at Perth. He deemed that it was the best he had ever bowled, and he could have taken 10 wickets in an innings had Michael Kasprowicz not snared the final two. For the second time, an eight-for from McGrath represented the best innings figures by an Australian in a Test since Mailey's nine-for in 1920-21. McGrath then took 18 wickets in three Tests as Australia again beat the Kiwis, before entering the 2005 Ashes series on 499 Test wickets.

McGrath's double of 5-53 and 4-29 helped Australia to a 239-run win in the first Test at Lord's, but he was forced to miss the second Test after injuring his ankle in a freak mishap on the morning of day one. England won by an agonising two runs to level the series, then McGrath returned for the third Test and helped salvage a draw as England threatened to grab the series lead.

Injury troubles came back to plague McGrath, who missed the fourth Test with an elbow problem; England won by just five wickets after making Australia follow on. There was no point wondering what might have been had McGrath played in the two Tests that Australia lost before returning for the final Test, which Australia needed to win to keep hold of the Ashes urn for a record ninth successive series. McGrath took five wickets in the match to take his series tally to 19

wickets at 23.16, but a draw ensured England triumphed overall.

As McGrath recalled in *The Ashes: Match of My Life*: 'Those last few hours at The Oval were torture. I could hear the crowd singing and celebrating the return of the Ashes, champagne corks were popping all over the ground and every trip to the boundary forced me to come face-to-face with an army of gloating England fans. I now know what hell looks like! … Was losing the Ashes as horrible as I had imagined? It was worse. Much worse. I felt sick. I never wanted to be part of an Australian side who lost a series to England, but here I was on the field at The Oval watching Michael Vaughan and his team get their hands on the urn … We weren't robbed, we weren't unlucky, let there be no doubt England deserved to win the Ashes … we were caught out by an England side who took their game to the next level.'

In the same chapter, McGrath remarked: 'I played cricket as hard as anyone, but afterwards I liked to share a cold beer with the opposition and have a chat. That is the point of cricket and I wouldn't want it any other way. After all, it is only a game.'

McGrath (far right) with fellow pacemen Brett Lee and Andy Bichel after Australia thrashed the West Indies by an innings at the Gabba in November 2000. McGrath had staggering match figures of 10-27 from 33 overs.

Back home, McGrath took 2-34 and 1-8 in a one-off victory against a World XI before claiming 13 wickets in a 3-0 drubbing of the West Indies and a somewhat modest eight wickets in three Tests against South Africa. He missed the subsequent tours of South Africa and Bangladesh due to his wife Jane's battle with breast cancer, as Australia maintained its winning sequence since losing the 2005 Ashes.

McGrath's last hurrah in Tests was the 2006-07 Ashes on home soil; his international farewell was the 2007 World Cup in the Caribbean. With Australia winning the Ashes series 5-0, McGrath claimed 21 scalps at 23.90, and was one of four Australian bowlers to take between 20 and 26 wickets. His best innings figures were 6-50, and in his farewell Test in his home state he nabbed three wickets in each innings. For good measure, his final delivery in Test cricket produced a wicket. With Australia subsequently having another undefeated World Cup

McGrath makes a mess of Andrew Flintoff's stumps during an Ashes Test in England in 2005.

For good measure, his final delivery in Test cricket produced a wicket.

campaign, McGrath took 1-31 from seven overs against Sri Lanka in the final, having taken his sole wicket with his penultimate delivery.

A number 11 batsman, McGrath was dismissed first ball in his Test and one-day international debuts.

After averaging 2.11 with a highest score of 9 in his first 21 Tests, McGrath made 24 against the West Indies at Sydney and occasionally featured in a handy last-wicket partnership. Never expected to last long with the bat, he scored 61 against New Zealand at Brisbane in late 2004 and even hit a six.

McGrath developed a habit of publicly targeting opposition players, particularly the likes of Lara, in the lead-up to a Test series, and he would often back it up. His sledging sometimes gave the Australian team a bad look although he was by no means the only culprit. Among team-mates, McGrath was known to be a nuisance at times. As Ponting wrote in *At the Close of Play*: 'As a pest, he truly is second to none. He was deadly from 20 metres with a grape in his hand; he'd just flick the fruit and hit you behind the ear every time.'

After McGrath's wife Jane sadly lost her battle with breast cancer in June 2008, the formation of the McGrath Foundation ensured Glenn McGrath would be remembered for more than just his on-field results.

Career statistics

	Tests	One-day internationals	First-class matches
Matches	124	250	189
Innings	138	68	193
Not outs	51	38	67
Runs scored	641	115	977
Batting average	7.37	3.83	7.75
100s / 50s	0 / 1	0 / 0	0 / 2
Top score	61	11	61
Balls bowled	29,248	12,970	41,759
Runs	12,186	8,391	17,414
Wickets	563	381	835
Bowling average	21.64	22.02	20.86
5 wickets in an innings	29	7	42
10 wickets in a match	3	n/a	7
Best bowling	8/24 (10/27)	7 / 15	8 / 24
Catches	38	37	54

BIBLIOGRAPHY

BOOKS

Armstrong, Geoff. (2009). *The 100 Greatest Cricketers.* New Holland Publishers (Australia) Pty Ltd, Sydney.

Arnold, Peter. (1987). *The Illustrated Encyclopedia of World Cricket.* Golden Press, Sydney.

Austin, David and co. (1997). *200 Seasons of Australian Cricket.* Pan Macmillan Australia, Sydney.

Boon, David. (1996). *Under the Southern Cross.* HarperCollinsPublishers Pty Ltd, Sydney.

Border, Allan. (1986). *An Autobiography.* Methuen Australia Pty Ltd.

Border, Allan. (2014). *Cricket as I see it.* Allen & Unwin, Crows Nest, Sydney.

Border, Allan and co. (2000). *The Dominators: One of the greatest Test teams.* Hodder Headline Australia Pty Limited, Sydney.

Botham, Ian. (2001). *Botham's Century.* Collins Willow, London.

Crowe, Martin. (1995). *Out on a Limb.* Reed Publishing, Auckland.

Frith, David. (1993). *Australia versus England: A pictorial history of every Test match since 1877.* Richard Smart Publishing, Sydney.

Gilchrist, Adam. (2008). *True Colours.* Pan Macmillan Australia, Sydney.

Gower, David. (2015). *David Gower's 50 Greatest Cricketers of All Time.* Icon Books Ltd, London.

Hauser, Liam. (2013). *A Century of Cricket Tests.* New Holland Publishers (Australia) Pty Ltd, Sydney.

Hauser, Liam. (2016). *A History of Test Cricket.* New Holland Publishers (Australia) Pty Ltd, Sydney.

Hayden, Matthew. (2010). *Standing My Ground.* Penguin Group (Australia), Camberwell, Victoria.

Imran Khan. (1988). *All Round View.* Chatto and Windus, London.

McGrath, Glenn and Lane, Daniel. (2008). *Glenn McGrath: Line and Strength.* Random House Australia Pty Ltd, Sydney.

Meher-Homji, Kersi. (2008). *Cricket's Great All-rounders.* New Holland Publishers (Australia) Pty Ltd, Sydney.

Miller, Allan. *Allan's Australian Cricket Annual,* self-published. 1987-88, 1988-89, 1989-90, 1990-91, 1991-92, 1992-93, 1993-94, 1994-95, 1996, 1997, 1998, 1999, 2000, 2001.

Perry, Roland. (2002). *Bradman's Best Ashes Teams.* Random House Australia Pty Ltd, Milsons Point, Sydney.

Pilger, Sam and Wightman, Rob. (2013). *The Ashes: Match of my life.* Pitch Publishing, Durrington.

Ponting, Ricky and Staples, Peter. (1998). *Punter: First Tests of a Champion.* Pan Macmillan Australia, Sydney.

Ponting, Ricky. (2013). *Ponting: At the Close of Play.* HarperCollins Publishers, Sydney.

Rippon, Anton. (1982). *Classic Moments of the Ashes.* Moorland Publishing, Derbyshire.

Sobers, Garry. (2002). *My Autobiography.* Headline Book Publishing, London.

Taylor, Mark. (1995). *Taylor Made.* Pan Macmillan Australia, Sydney.

Waugh, Steve. (1994). *Steve Waugh's South African Tour Diary.* Pan Macmillan Australia, Sydney.

Waugh, Steve. (1995). *Steve Waugh's West Indies Tour Diary.* HarperCollins Publishers Pty Ltd, Sydney.

Waugh, Steve. (1997). *Steve Waugh's 1997 Ashes Diary.* HarperCollins Publishers Pty Ltd, Sydney.

Waugh, Steve. (2005). *Out of My Comfort Zone: The autobiography.* Penguin Group (Australia).

Willis, Bob. (1996). *Six of the Best.* Hodder and Stoughton Ltd, London.

NEWSPAPERS

Courier-Mail
Daily Telegraph
Herald Sun
New Zealand Herald
Sydney Morning Herald
WA Today

INTERNET

cricket.com.au
ESPNcricinfo
foxsports.com.au
news.com.au (12/5/16: 'Justin Langer, Matthew Hayden defend Steve Waugh after Shane Warne's comments')
theroar.com.au
Wikipedia
http://www.watoday.com.au/wa-news/dennis-lillees-search-for-his-greatest-inspiration-his-primary-school-teacher-20161110-gsmnri.html
http://www.watoday.com.au/wa-news/dennis-lillee-set-to-be-reunited-with-beloved-school-teacher-after-6pr-appeal-20161111-gsn76v.html
http://www.cricketcountry.com/articles/cricketing-rifts-1-the-bradman-centric-and-religion-fuelled-australian-feuds-11838
http://www.cricketcountry.com/articles/keith-milller-34-facts-about-the-golden-boy-of-australian-cricket-510419
http://www.abc.net.au/austory/the-millers-tale—part-1/9172986
http://www.abc.net.au/austory/content/2007/s2549767.htm
http://www.abc.net.au/7.30/content/2004/s1218626.htm

ABOUT THE AUTHOR

Liam Hauser developed a strong interest in cricket and rugby league while in primary school, and has supported and read about those two sports ever since. Not possessing the prowess to play sport at an elite level, he decided instead to write about it – beginning with fictional cricket and rugby league stories before turning to writing about the real thing.

During his Bachelor of Journalism course at Queensland University of Technology he gained practical experience with radio, television, print and online media. Upon completing his degree he landed his first journalism position as a sports reporter at the *South Burnett Times* in Kingaroy, subsequently working also for the *Tumut and Adelong Times*, the *Gundagai Independent* and the *Tumbarumba Times*.

Liam concentrated on book writing for much of 2017 before working as a commercial features editor at *The Northern Star* in late 2017 and early 2018. His previous books include *State of Origin 35 Years* (Rockpool, 2015); *A Century of Cricket Tests* (2013); *A History of Test Cricket* (2016); and *The Great Grand Finals: Rugby League's Greatest Contests* (2017).

Over the years Liam has written about many sports including cricket, rugby league, rugby union, oztag, touch football, soccer, gymnastics, campdrafting, equestrian, tennis, bowls, boxing, hockey, golf, rifle shooting, horse racing and archery. He has been interviewed on radio many times, particularly as an expert on subjects such as State of Origin rugby league.

MATTHEW HAYDEN · ARTHUR MORRIS ·
LAN BORDER · STEVE WAUGH · ADAM
ARNE · DENNIS LILLEE · GLENN McGR
ORRIS · DON BRADMAN · RICKY PONT
ADAM GILCHRIST · KEITH MILLER · SH
CGRATH · MATTHEW HAYDEN · ARTHUR
ONTING · ALLAN BORDER · STEVE WAU
· SHANE WARNE · DENNIS LILLEE · GL
THUR MORRIS · DON BRADMAN · RIC
AUGH · ADAM GILCHRIST · KEITH MIL
LENN McGRATH · MATTHEW HAYDEN
AN · RICKY PONTING · ALLAN BORDER
EITH MILLER · SHANE WARNE · DENN
EW HAYDEN · ARTHUR MORRIS · DON
RDER · STEVE WAUGH · ADAM GILCHF
ENNIS LILLEE · GLENN McGRATH · M
S DON BRADMAN · RICKY PONTING
AM GILCHRIST · KEITH MILLER · SHAI
CGRATH · MATTHEW HAYDEN · ARTHU
NTING · ALLAN BORDER · STEVE WAU
· SHANE WARNE · DENNIS LILLEE · GL
THUR MORRIS · DON BRADMAN · RIC

MATTHEW HAYDEN · ARTHUR MORRIS ·
AN BORDER · STEVE WAUGH · ADAM G
ENNIS LILLEE · GLENN MCGRATH · MA
RADMAN · RICKY PONTING · ALLAN BO
KEITH MILLER · SHANE WARNE · DENN
AYDEN · ARTHUR MORRIS · DON BRAD
TEVE WAUGH · ADAM GILCHRIST · KEIT
GLENN MCGRATH · MATTHEW HAYDEN
ICKY PONTING · ALLAN BORDER · STE
R · SHANE WARNE · DENNIS LILLEE · G
HUR MORRIS · DON BRADMAN · RICKY
ADAM GILCHRIST · KEITH MILLER · SH
RATH · MATTHEW HAYDEN · ARTHUR M
LLAN BORDER · STEVE WAUGH · ADAM
DENNIS LILLEE · GLENN MCGRATH · M
RADMAN · RICKY PONTING · ALLAN BO
KEITH MILLER · SHANE WARNE · DENN
AYDEN · ARTHUR MORRIS · DON BRAD
TEVE WAUGH · ADAM GILCHRIST · KEIT
GLENN MCGRATH · MATTHEW HAYDEN
ICKY PONTING · ALLAN BORDER · STE
R · SHANE WARNE · DENNIS LILLEE ·